TWELVE PROPHETIC VOICES

TWELVE PROPHETIC VOICES

MARIANO DiGANGI

While this book is designed for your personal profit and enjoyment, it is also intended for group study. A Leader's Guide with Victor Multiuse Transparency Masters is available from your local bookstore or from the publisher.

VICTOR

BOOKS a division of SP Publications, Inc.
WHEATON. ILLINOIS 60187

Offices also in
Whitby, Ontario, Canada
Amersham-on-the-Hill, Bucks, England

All Scripture quotations are from the *Holy Bible: New International Version,* © 1973, 1978, 1984 by the International Bible Society. Used by permission of Zondervan Bible Publishers.

Recommended Dewey Decimal Classification: 224.9
Suggested Subject Heading: MINOR PROPHETS

Library of Congress Catalog Card Number: 85-50315
ISBN: 0-89693-536-1

VICTOR BOOKS
A division of SP Publications, Inc.
        Wheaton, Illinois 60187

CONTENTS

PROLOGUE

We are witnessing the collapse of a civilization. Idealism is giving way to cynicism. Radicals and reactionaries polarize society. The values of our Judeo-Christian tradition are thoughtlessly bartered for a mess of relativistic pottage. Material affluence has not bought us happiness, but only increased our greed and deepened our boredom. Violence, vice, anxiety, and agony are facts of national and international life. The perversion of sexuality, the brutality of child abuse, the painful estrangement of shattering divorce—all signal the death of the family. The notion of our innate goodness and the myth of inevitable technological progress lie like limp and livid corpses on the stage of contemporary history.

The predicament of humanity is, unfortunately, intensified by the state of the church. True, there are instances of evangelistic advance, particularly in Latin America and Africa south of the Sahara. Here and there, some congregations are experiencing renewal as Word and Spirit combine to bring repentance and new life. But the majority opinion is that the body of Christ is in decline. The rituals continue and budgets are met. Yet the church is increasingly irrelevant to the process by which many people make the major decisions of life. It has generally lost the moral authority thought indispensable to serving as the conscience of the nation. Unless spiritual recovery occurs in the church, how can the world be spared from impending catastrophe?

But we must press this question beyond the world, beyond the church, to ourselves. Are we, as individuals, guilty of paying mere lip service to the evangelical doctrines and moral principles of Christianity? Is our religion one of form without substance, emotion divorced from the great facts of redemptive history, a resolve that dies stillborn? When faced with our personal mortality, do we come to terms with death in the awareness of the Resurrection and the Life? Or do we surrender to unreasoning panic when confronted with man's last enemy?

It is high time we examine our standards in the light of an absolute standard, weigh our innermost motives, and evaluate the goals for which we strive. It is high time we reacquaint ourselves with God. The true and living God is no deaf or dumb nonentity. He has left clues of Himself in the created universe. "Since the creation of the world God's invisible qualities—His eternal power and divine nature—have been clearly seen, being understood from what has been made, so that men are without excuse" if they suppress this natural knowledge of God (Rom. 1:20). God has, moreover, revealed something of His will in the human conscience. Even pagans lacking biblical revelation "do by nature things required by the Law . . . since they show that the requirements of the Law are written on their hearts, their consciences also bearing witness, and their thoughts now accusing, now even defending them" (Rom. 2:14-15). It is in His Word, however, that God has given us the revelation we most desperately need.

We are not merely creatures who contemplate God's general revelation in the created world or consider what we hear in our consciences. We are sinners in need of a special disclosure that can bring about our spiritual recovery. Only because God has spoken to us in His Word can we know with clarity and certainty the truth about the Deity, the duty He requires of us, the depth of our depravity, the dignity that may be ours by His grace, and the glorious destiny that awaits the people of God. We understand, therefore, the necessity of Holy Scripture. "For everything that was written in the past was written to teach us, so that through endurance and the encouragement of the Scriptures we might have hope" (Rom. 15:4).

The focal point of biblical revelation is Jesus Christ. To Him do the prophets and apostles bear witness. "These are the Scriptures that testify about Me" (John 5:39), He says. In the writings of "Moses and all the Prophets," we should look, then, for that which tells us of His sufferings and His glory (Luke 24:25-27).

The minor prophets are an integral part of the revelational process whose climax is Jesus Christ, the Word made flesh: "In the past God spoke to our forefathers through the prophets at many times and in various ways, but in these last days He has spoken to us by His Son" (Heb. 1:1-2). The prophets prepared the way for the Way, summoning people to repentance and announcing the advent of the Redeemer. The apostles affirmed that Jesus was the Messiah of whom the prophets spoke. They showed how His atoning death and mighty resurrection fulfilled the promises in the prophetic writings (Acts 2:22-36; 1 Cor. 15:3-4).

The prophets, however, are not revelational robots. The Spirit of God neither obliterates their personalities nor renders them oblivious to the conditions around them. The prophets speak out of their own particular set of circumstances and in their own individual styles. Yet no prophetic Scripture originated in the fertile imagination of any prophet. As Peter notes: "For prophecy never had its origin in the will of man, but men spoke from God as they were carried along by the Holy Spirit" (2 Peter 1:21). That is why Paul affirms the inspiration and authority of the Old Testament writings, of which the minor prophets form so vital a part: "All Scripture is God-breathed and is useful for teaching, rebuking, correcting, and training in righteousness, so that the man of God may be thoroughly equipped for every good work" (2 Tim. 3:16-17).

When we refer to the prophets, we also should remember some basic distinctions. Scripture separates true prophets from false. The false prophet is a windbag who has been given nothing to say, but says it most impressively. The true prophet is a spokesman for God. Called of the Lord, cleansed by His grace, committed to the communication of the Word, the genuine prophet is a mouthpiece for God. He puts his ear to the chest of the Eternal, catches something of His heartbeat, and shares what he has heard with the Lord's people.

Scripture mentions some nonwriting prophets, such as Elijah and Elisha. The writing prophets, though, have been classified as major (Isaiah, Jeremiah, and Ezekiel) and minor. This latter category comprises Hosea, Joel, Amos, Obadiah, Jonah, Micah, Nahum, Habakkuk, Zephaniah, Haggai, Zechariah, and Malachi. Sometimes referred to as "The Twelve," they are termed "minor" only because of the comparative brevity of their writings. In actuality, they deal with some very major themes. If you are listening for some lighthearted *scherzo* or trivial minuet, you won't find it here. In these writings, like the rest of Scripture, we can hear the vibrant voice of the living God.

The true prophet shows both insight and foresight. By foresight, I refer to the reality of predictive prophecy. Rationalism denies the possibility of such prophecy, and reconstructs Scripture so as to obscure or obviate the connection between prophecy and fulfillment. Yet if we take biblical revelation seriously, we will see that what is spoken by the prophets comes to pass in the course of history. The New Testament Gospels abound in such fulfillment, and we are grateful to the sovereign God who faithfully keeps His promises.

But even those persons who admit that predictive prophecy *can* occur, may mistreat and distort the Word. This happens whenever prophecy is allegorized or reduced to inappropriate symbolism. When interpreting sacred writings, we need an exposition of truth, not the imposition of personal biases.

In studying biblical prophecy, we also must give careful attention to the dynamic interrelation between eschatological, evangelical, and ethical elements. This is but to recognize that the words of the prophets not only foretell, but tell forth. They not only predict the future, but reveal God's will regarding the present. They herald the advent of the Messiah and emphasize the need for integrity in our social, political, and economic relationships. They declare that Christ comes to liberate His people from the condemnation and corruption of sin, and summon believers to live in a way that demonstrates this messianic freedom.

Any view of prophecy which fails to focus on the centrality of Him whose unique Person and work are at the heart of the evangel, or which encourages escape from contemporary ethical responsibility, violates the integrity of the inspired Word. Such misinterpretation appreciates neither the predictions nor perceptions of the prophets.

Peter once wrote about "ignorant and unstable people" who "distort . . . the . . . Scriptures to their own destruction" (2 Peter 3:16). May we willingly let the Spirit guide us into a right understanding of the truths and duties revealed in these prophetic writings.

DEDICATION

To the faculty and students of
Ontario Theological Seminary,
a company committed to
understanding,
expounding, and obeying
God's inspired
and infallible Word.

"Blessed Lord, who hast
caused all Holy Scriptures
to be written for our
learning; grant that we
may in such wise hear
them, read, mark, learn, and
inwardly digest them,
that by patience, and
comfort of Thy holy Word,
we may embrace, and ever
hold fast the blessed
hope of everlasting life, which
Thou hast given us in our
Saviour Jesus Christ,
Amen."
COLLECT FOR THE SECOND SUNDAY IN
ADVENT

ONE

"This Prophet's Commission is chiefly to Israel, and therefore he speaks but little to Judah; and albeit these Tribes after their rent and defection from David's Family did also make Apostasie from the true Worship of God, he comforts the godly with Predictions of Gospel mercies, and particularly, with Promises of the Conversion of that Nation, and of God's renewing Covenant with them, after their long rejection and sequestration" (George Hutcheson, A BRIEF EXPOSITION ON THE TWELVE SMALL PROPHETS, Ralph Smith, p. 1).

"The distinctive element is to be found in Hosea's use of the Hebrew word *chesed*, usually translated by 'mercy' or 'loving-kindness.' The word stands for God's steadfast love for the people of His choice, for the Israel with whom He had made a covenant" (Davies, Richardson, and Wallis, eds., THE TWENTIETH CENTURY BIBLE COMMENTARY, Harper & Brothers, p. 301).

"It is as if God purposed to Himself two things: first that a book should be found in His Writ that was to proclaim His Mercy and His Love before any of His other attributes; and second that a prophet should be raised up to write that book in the scorching tears of his own shame" (Hubert Van Zeller, THE OUTSPOKEN ONES, Sheed & Ward, p. 8).

"He was taught the truth of the tenderness of the Divine heart by the command of Jehovah to love, and find, and restore his sinful bride. Through his obedience he entered into fellowship with the amazing tenderness of God," (G. Campbell Morgan, THE ANALYZED BIBLE, F.H. Revell, pp. 274-275).

HOSEA
A LOVE STORY

YOU CAN READ about it in the daily newspaper, hear about it on the evening news. It is a disease which has reached epidemic proportions. Like any disease, its causes are sometimes difficult to diagnose; difficult, but not impossible. The fact is, the illness of divorce often can be traced to the simple failure of men and women to understand what true commitment is all about, to appreciate the value of meaningful relationships.

The Book of Hosea deals with these very matters: broken commitments and shattered relationships. It also points the way to redemption and reconciliation. Hosea, more than any other prophet, speaks with pathos and passion about the loving-kindness of the Lord to a wayward and—in every sense of the word—adulterous people.

The complex prophecy of Hosea can be considered thematically along these lines:

(1) A Meaningful Relationship
   A. Man and Wife (1:2)
   B. Lord and People (1:2)

(2) A Broken Relationship
   A. Ingratitude (2:8; 4:1, 6; 8:14; 5:4; 13:4-6)

B. Idolatry (4:17; 5:4; 8:4-6; 10:5-6)
C. Infidelity (7:11, 13; 8:9, 11-14; 6:4-10)
D. Injustice (4:1-2; 7:1-15)

(3) A Restored Relationship
A. Apostasy Deserves Discipline (1:4, 6, 8; 2:1-5, 13; 4:14; 8:1—10:15)
B. Discipline Serves Grace (5:15)
C. Grace Encourages Reconciliation (2:14-23; 3:1-5; 5:15; 13:14; 6:1-6; 12:6; 14:1-9)

A MEANINGFUL RELATIONSHIP

Man and Wife. At the very outset of his book, Hosea refers to marriage (1:2). As this subject will prove to be a central theme of Hosea's prophecy, it would seem wise to briefly review what the Bible teaches about marriage.

Because God made us male and female, our sexuality clearly is a part of His creation. Yet He has ordained that the fulfillment of sexual desire occur *within* marriage for the mutual enjoyment of husband and wife, as well as for the procreation of children. According to the divine plan, "a man will leave his father and mother and be united to his wife, and they may become one flesh" (Gen. 2:24).

For the Christian, the transforming power of God's saving grace further enriches the marriage relationship. Out of a common connection to Him who is Saviour and Lord, husband and wife are encouraged to deal with each other lovingly. Writing to a community of disciples in Asia Minor, the Apostle Paul declared:

> Wives, submit yourselves to your husbands, as is fitting in the Lord. Husbands, love your wives and do not be harsh with them (Col. 3:18-19).

Lord and people. The marriage relationship between husbands and wives also should remind us of the union between the Lord and His people. He unites them with Himself in a covenant of love.

In the Old Testament, God's relationship to Israel often is described in terms of marriage. Speaking for Jehovah, Isaiah said:

> Your Maker is your husband—
> the Lord Almighty is His name—
> the Holy One of Israel is your Redeemer;
> He is called the God of all the earth
> (Isa. 54:5).

In the New Testament, Paul further develops the marriage analogy between God and man. Recall his words to the community at Ephesus:

> Wives, submit to your husbands as to the Lord. For the husband is the head of the wife as Christ is the head of the church, His body, of which He is the Saviour. Now as the church submits to Christ, so also wives should submit to their husbands in everything.
> Husbands, love your wives, just as Christ loved the church and gave Himself up for her to make her holy, cleansing her by the washing with water through the word, and to present her to Himself as a radiant church, without stain or wrinkle or any other blemish, but holy and blameless (Eph. 5:22-27).

It also is important to note that God is revealed as "a jealous God" (Ex. 20:5; Deut. 5:9). In other words, He loves His people so intensely that no rival can be tolerated. For Israel to break their covenant relationship with Him would be to commit spiritual adultery—forsaking the true God—to go after false gods.

My reason for this review of Scripture is basic. In a day and age when cynics depreciate marriage and misguided sensuality defiles it, we need to recover something of the profound meaning of the wonderful marriage relationship. We must experience afresh something of the wonder of union and communion that exists between the Lord and His people. An acknowledgment of this view is at the very heart of Hosea's message, for he prophesied when Uzziah, Jotham, Ahaz, and Hezekiah ruled in Judah, and Jereboam, the son of Joash, reigned in Israel. Those were decades when God's people had thoroughly lost an appreciation for their relationship with the Almighty.

A BROKEN RELATIONSHIP

Ironically, Hosea experiences the bitter sting of faithlessness in his own life. Scripture indicates that the Lord told him to marry a prostitute (Hosea 1:2).

While numerous commentators have disagreed over whether this domestic tragedy actually happened to Hosea, one point remains strikingly clear. Just as Hosea experienced anguish at his wife's faithlessness, so too was God deeply hurt by Israel, a nation "guilty of the vilest adultery in departing from the Lord" (Hosea 1:2). Instead of being loyal to the Lord, bound with ties of gratitude and love, Israel turned away from Him and became infatuated with worthless paramours.

Ingratitude. Hosea notes that the Lord of the covenant has blessed the people with grain, new wine, and oil. He has enriched the land with gold and silver. But disloyal Israel has not acknowledged God as its benefactor (2:8). It has, instead, squandered His gifts on the worship of Baal—a pagan idol.

In their reckless pursuit of foreign gods, the people even have suppressed the knowledge of God offered to them in the Law and the Prophets:

There is no faithfulness, no love, no acknowledgment of God in the land (4:1).

Seeing this, the Lord justly complains:

My people are destroyed from lack of knowledge (4:6).

The tragic truth is, "Israel has forgotten his Maker" (8:14) and the priests of the people "do not acknowledge the Lord" (5:4). The Lord amplifies His charges against Israel in sorrowful words:

I am the Lord your God, who brought you out of Egypt. You shall acknowledge no God but Me, no Saviour except Me. I cared for you in the desert, in the land of burning heat. When I fed them, they were satisfied; when they were satisfied, they became proud; then they forgot Me (13:4-6).

Regrettably, these same words could be addressed to professing Christians today. If we allow possessions or positions to come before our relationship with God, we too have become spiritual adulterers.

Idolatry. Baal and Astoreth were among the gods worshiped in the heathen environment surrounding Israel. Baal was pictured as a male sky god, while Astoreth was portrayed as an earth goddess. The cult of these divinities featured orgiastic rites—involving prostitution at the shrines—which were thought to increase the fertility of the land. The real result of these rituals, however, was the spread of immorality.

The kingdom of Israel, also known as Ephraim or Samaria, began to adopt and embrace these pagan ways. Vulnerable to illusions, prey to seductions and deceptions, "Ephraim is joined to idols" (4:17). But God's spokesman, Hosea, exposes the sin of the Israelites boldly:

> Their deeds do not permit them to return to their God. A spirit of prostitution is in their heart; they do not acknowledge the Lord (5:4).

> With their silver and gold they make idols for themselves to their own destruction. Throw out your calf-idol, O Samaria! My anger burns against them. How long will they be incapable of purity? They are from Israel! This calf—a craftsman has made it; it is not God. It will be broken in pieces, that calf of Samaria (8:4-6).

Prophetically, Hosea notes that the day will come when the idol that has displaced the only true God in the affections of His people will be carried away to Assyria. Then Israel will be disgraced and ashamed of its false gods (10:5-6).

Hosea's comments concerning idolatry are extremely important. Consider Martin Luther's observations on this topic:

> It is very easy to fall into idolatry, for all of us are idolaters by nature. . . . In reality, the heathen make their own fictitious notions and dreams of God an idol and rely on what is altogether nothing. That is what all idolatry is. It consists not merely in erecting an image and worshiping it. Its seat is in the heart, which stupidly stares in other directions

and seeks help and comfort from creatures, saints or devils
.... Not only the adoration of images is idolatry but also
trust in one's own righteousness, works, and merits, and
putting confidence in riches and human power.... How
godless do you think it is to rely on these things and to
reject confidence in the eternal and omnipotent God?
(*What Luther Says*, E.M. Plass, ed., Concordia, vol. 2, pp.
678-679).

Infidelity. God now confronts Israel's shocking faithlessness. Instead of trusting and obeying God, "Ephraim is like a
dove, easily deceived and senseless—now calling to Egypt,
now turning to Assyria" for help (Hosea 7:11). But those who
stray from God will meet with misery, Hosea states, and all
who rebel against Him face sure destruction (7:13). The
Northern Kingdom "has sold herself to lovers" at whose
hands it will experience cruelty (8:9). Ephraim has built
many altars for sin offerings, but these have become altars for
sinning as God's worship is adulterated through the introduction of idolatry and immorality.

All these actions are not without consequences. They kin-
dle the fire of God's displeasure and will result in punishment; specifically, Israel will again endure defeat and enslavement (8:11-14). More on this in a moment.

Hosea's main point here is that to profess allegiance to the
Lord, and then to let love vanish like the morning mist, is
nothing less than betrayal. It defiles the traitor and disgusts
the betrayed (6:4-10). Even today, it is easy for us to sing, "O
Jesus I have promised to serve Thee to the end." But staying
true to that promise, when the pressure to compromise moral
principles is felt, can be much more difficult. Obviously, Israel has failed this test. Have we?

Injustice. In light of these developments, Hosea courageously delivers the message God has given him. Listen to his
ringing indictment of the people:

Hear the word of the Lord, you Israelites, because the Lord
has a charge to bring against you who live in the land:
There is no faithfulness, no love, no acknowledgment of
God in the land. There is only cursing, lying and murder,

stealing and adultery; they break all bounds, and blood-shed follows bloodshed (4:1-2).

Hosea, in essence, has summarized the results of Israel's apostasy. Justice is driven away and the social order is thrown into confusion. Deceit is common. Thieves break into homes and bandits rob in the streets. Ambush and murder await the unsuspecting. And what is the source of the radical evil from which such injustice grows? Quite simply, it is man's stubborn rejection of God's moral law (7:1-15). The dreadful result of breaking His covenant and disobeying His commands is not self-fulfillment, but the loss of dignity and freedom.

A RESTORED RELATIONSHIP

Hosea now begins to address the issue of how Israel can restore its relationship with God. But first, he makes several additional comments about why the nation has found itself in such dire straits.

Basically, the very leaders who were to serve as guides for the people wound up misleading them. The "prophets" have stumbled (4:5-6) and the priests have rejected knowledge, ignored the Law of God, sinned against the Lord, and traded the worship of God for disgraceful idolatry (4:6-8). As a result, the people are destroyed from a lack of knowledge concerning what is right and wrong.

Seeing this, the Lord declares His intention: "I will punish both of them for their ways and repay them for their deeds" (4:9).

Apostasy Deserves Discipline. Three children were born to Hosea and Gomer; their names are significant in that they reveal how God will discipline His people. First, a son named Jezreel was born; his name foretold punishment for the house of Jehu and an end to the kingdom of Israel. The Lord had not forgotten the atrocity committed by Ahab and Jezebel against Naboth at Jezreel (Hosea 1:4; 1 Kings 21).

The second child, a daughter, was named Lo-Ruhamah— "She Is Not Pitied"—symbolizing the end of all mercy for Israel (Hosea 1:6).

The third child, Lo-Ammi, signified that Israel would become "Not My People" (1:8). Those who persist in rejecting the Lord are deserving of rejection and discipline.

The Lord again rebukes the unfaithful in His displeasure and warns:

> I will make her like a desert, turn her into a parched land, and slay her with thirst. I will not show My love to her children, because they are the children of adultery. Their mother has been unfaithful and has conceived them in disgrace (2:3-5).

> I will punish her for the days she burned incense to the Baals (2:13).

> A people without understanding will come to ruin! (4:14)

This theme is developed throughout the fifth chapter of Hosea's prophecy and is repeated in the eighth. God says that Israel is doomed to "reap the whirlwind" because "the people have broken My covenant and rebelled against My Law" (8:1). If we dare to break God's moral law, it will break us. We cannot sin with impunity.

The ninth chapter continues God's indictment of Israel and warns of judgment:

> The days of punishment are coming,
> the days of reckoning are at hand.
> Let Israel know this (9:7).

We know now that Israel eventually was defeated and deported to Assyria (2 Kings 15:29; 17:6); here, Hosea points ominously to that very development:

> My God will reject them because they have not obeyed Him; they will be wanderers among the nations (Hosea 9:17).

> Their heart is deceitful, and now they must bear their guilt. The Lord will demolish their altars and destroy their sacred stones (10:2).

We never should assume that these stern words apply only

to the Israelites of Hosea's time. They are relevant to all who claim a relationship with the Lord, but who live as though He either did not exist, or that His existence didn't really matter.

Discipline Serves Grace. If God disciplines His people, it is not only to demonstrate a righteous indignation against moral evil; it is to bring Israel to the point of brokenness and repentance. The Lord says that He will turn away from the covenant breakers *until* they admit their guilt, seek His face, and from the depths of their misery cry out to Him for help (5:15). Discipline thus serves the purpose of grace.

The humbling experiences of life, those which expose the folly of our wisdom and the weakness of our strength, may be used of God for good—*if* they lead us to Him who alone can save. The chastisements we endure should not be despised. Rather, they should motivate us to renounce all pride and honestly express penitence. This is God's gracious purpose.

A chastened disciple knows that "the Lord disciplines those He loves, and He punishes everyone He accepts as a son" (Heb. 12:6). We should humble ourselves under God's mighty hand, since He "disciplines us for our own good, that we may share His holiness" (12:10).

Grace Encourages Reconciliation. When we understand that God disciplines us for our own good, we become aware of His grace and are encouraged to take the steps of repentance and faith necessary to bring us back to the Lord.

Through Hosea's prophecy, God reveals His gracious purpose regarding wayward Israel. He promises to lead her into the desert and speak tenderly to His people. He offers Israel fresh hope, renewed prosperity, and the recovery of the joy the people experienced at the time of the Exodus (Hosea 2:14-15). On that day, Israel will again acknowledge Him as her husband and will turn away from false lovers. Conflict no longer will engulf the nation, but security, righteousness, justice, love, compassion, and faithfulness will flow forth (2:16-20). Then, those who have been estranged from God will experience a new covenant relationship with Him (2:21-23).

Symbolic of this renewed relationship, the Lord tells Hosea to show his love to Gomer once again, even though she has been unfaithful to him (3:1-5). He is to love her as the Lord loves the Israelites who have turned to other gods and corrupted their worship. After redeeming her, Hosea takes Gomer home to live with him once more.

This action represents God's redemptive work with the Israelites, who "will live many days without king or prince, without sacrifice or sacred stones, without ephod or idol" (3:4). Afterward, "the Israelites will return and seek the Lord their God. . . . They will come trembling to the Lord and to His blessings in the last days" (3:5).

When the people admit their guilt and seek God's face, then He will turn to them in welcoming grace (5:15). The Lord will not give up His people, nor will He deal with them as He treated Admah and Zeboiim or Sodom and Gomorrah (Gen. 10:19; 19:24-25; Deut. 29:23).

Now, "all of the compassions and mercies of the infinite God burst out into full flame, consuming the fierceness of His anger, burning unto the lowest hell" (Theodore Laetsch, *The Minor Prophets*, Concordia, p. 91). The Lord promises to restore His people from the oppression of Egypt and the might of Assyria. Moreover, He promises:

> I will ransom them from the power of the grave; I will redeem them from death. Where, O death, are your plagues? Where, O grave, is your destruction? (Hosea 13:14)

Because the Lord is gracious, penitent people in every generation may confidently say:

> Come let us return to the Lord. He has torn us to pieces but He will heal us; He has injured us but He will bind up our wounds. After two days He will revive us; on the third day He will restore us, that we may live in His presence. Let us acknowledge the Lord; let us press on to acknowledge Him. As surely as the sun rises, He will appear; He will come to us like the winter rains, like the spring rains that water the earth" (6:1-3).

Our response to God's grace must be that of real repentance. We must not offer Him a superficial penance which involves only the external rituals of religion. The Lord's demand is definite:

I desire mercy, not sacrifice, and acknowledgment of God rather than burnt offerings (6:6).

What does this command imply? For one, God looks for more than the performance of formal worship. He desires that we do justly, love mercy, and walk humbly with Him day by day.

Through His servant, the Lord further explains these standards:

You must return to your God; maintain love and justice, and wait for your God always (12:6).

Return, O Israel, to the Lord your God. Your sins have been your downfall! . . . Say to Him: "Forgive all our sins and receive us graciously, that we may offer the fruit of our lips. . . . We will never again say 'Our gods' to what our own hands have made, for in You the fatherless find compassion" (14:1-3).

There *is* a way back to God. We may confidently take it, believing that the Lord of sovereign grace has opened a door of hope for us and will receive us with the warm welcome of His loving heart. This is God's own promise:

I will heal their waywardness and love them freely, for My anger has turned away from them (14:4).

He will refresh us like the morning dew, cause us to grow as cedars of Lebanon, and make us fruitful (14:5-8).

The wise person will realize the truth of what the Prophet Hosea has said. The discerning individual will understand both the warnings of God's justice and the promises of His grace, and act accordingly (14:9). This is the way to new life and strength, to spiritual renewal and everlasting salvation.

TWO

"Joel was the vehicle of a divine revelation which has a significance perhaps beyond his full understanding. In his book the impinging of the eternal on the temporal, which is the hallmark of genuine inspiration, is undeniably much in evidence.... One of the most disturbing and heart-searching books of the Old Testament" (J.D. Young, ed., THE NEW BIBLE DICTIONARY, IVP, p. 639).

"Joel's purpose is to warn the nation of the need for humility and repentance and the certainty of coming judgment. At the same time, he seeks to keep the heart of the people faithful to the promises of God by reminding them of the coming salvation and of the destruction of their and God's enemies" (E.J. Young, AN INTRODUCTION TO THE OLD TESTAMENT, Eerdmans, p. 273).

"Using a graphic style and a staccato rhythm, Joel describes the scene in the valley of decision. His disclosure of final judgment is designed to cause the impenitent dread, and bring the troubled people of God great comfort" (Mariano DiGangi, THE BOOK OF JOEL, Baker, p. 66).

"He reproves the stupidity of the people, who, when severely smitten by God, did not feel their evils, but on the contrary grew hardened under them.... He exhorts the people to repentance ... and bids them come as suppliants with tears. ... He prophesies of the Kingdom of Christ, and shows that though now all things seem full of despair, yet God had not forgotten the Covenant He made with the fathers; and that therefore Christ would come to gather the scattered remnants" (John Calvin, COMMENTARIES ON THE MINOR PROPHETS, John Owen, trans., Calvin Translation Society, vol. 1, p. xvi).

JOEL
PROPHET OF
PENTECOST

LIKE THE FIRST-CENTURY CHURCH AT CORINTH, the contemporary church is experiencing controversy and confusion over things charismatic. Is the gift of tongues, for instance, the only infallible evidence of being baptized in the Holy Spirit? Are you forever doomed to the agony of second-rate Christianhood unless you know the ecstasy of glossolalia? Or is this gift no longer operative? Should "charismatics" be considered psychologically unbalanced—perhaps even demon possessed?

The events which occurred at the first Pentecost following Easter—the very events which ignited this controversy—actually were a fulfillment of a prophecy made by Joel. But that prophecy comprised only one small part of the rich message contained in this book. In fact, Joel's message deals with three main themes: punishment, penitence, and promise. We should, therefore, take a fresh look at his book to see its pentecostal aspect in the context of all that the Spirit inspired Joel to prophesy.

(1) **Punishment**
   A. Disobedience (3:1-8; 1:5; 2:12-13; 3:21)
   B. Desolation (3:9-17; 1:1-12; 2:1-11)

(2) Penitence
  A. God's Call (1:13-14; 1:15-20)
  B. God's Demand (2:13, 15; 2:12-17)
  C. God's Encouragement (2:13-14)

(3) Promise
  A. The Spirit (2:28-29)
  B. The Saviour (2:30-32)
  C. The Nations Judged (3:1-16)
  D. The People Blessed (3:17-21)

PUNISHMENT

The first aspect of Joel's prophecy warns that those who are disobedient to God will be punished. Their future will be one of desolation.

Disobedience. Simply stated, sin consists of disobedience to God's moral law; it can be expressed by doing what He has forbidden, or by failing to do what He has commanded.

Joel specifically notes that the heathen nations surrounding Israel have disobeyed their Creator in a number of ways (3:1-8). They have cheapened human life and profaned His temple. They have scattered His people, divided up His land, traded boys for prostitutes, and sold girls for wine.

This disobedience, though, is not limited to the pagans. Even the covenant people come under indictment for their intemperance (1:5), their alienation from God (2:12-13), and their violence (3:21). And because Jerusalem has received a more clear and full revelation of God's will than the pagan peoples of the earth, it will be judged more severely for its disobedience.

Desolation. Because of their disobedience, God first will judge the heathen. Pagan oppressors will reckon with the One who rules the universe and calls every man to account. When He judges, none shall escape the eye of the Omniscient or intimidate the Omnipotent.

In every generation, there are always those few, foolish individuals who think they can outwit or defeat God. Yet Joel ridicules those who think they can escape judgment in this fashion. Let the mighty beat their plowshares into swords, he says, and their pruninghooks into spears. Let them try to engage the Eternal in combat. Let them face their inevitable encounter with the living God. But when God speaks in accents of judgment, the sun and moon shall be darkened and the stars shall shine no more (3:9-17). In symbolic terms, Joel has described the utter defeat of the pagans.

The covenant people—be they Israel or the church—are not immune to God's displeasure and discipline, either. Joel's prophecy shatters man's false security; he declares that God is about to let loose a dreadful invasion upon the land. Sometimes He allows wars or revolutions to chasten the nations. At other times, the Lord's word of judgment is put into effect through the forces of nature. So it is during the time of Joel's prophetic ministry. Millions of devouring and devastating insects will leave the land desolate. When God's impending judgment becomes an awesome reality, joy will give way to weeping, and the song of gladness will turn into howling despair (1:1-12).

Sound the alarm, Joel warns, and tremble as the Day of the Lord dawns with all its darkness and gloom. Israel—with a landscape once resembling Eden—shall rapidly be reduced to a desolate wilderness, as the plague of locust, palmerworm, cankerworm, and caterpillar comes from God to punish the sins of those who should have known better (2:1-11).

At the end of time, God again will reveal His wrath from heaven against the unrighteousness of men. The only way to flee from the punishment to come is revealed in the Gospel; Joel will have more to say on that blessed possibility in the course of his prophecy. But for now, let us understand that the God who punishes the nations for their sins will not exempt nominal and hypocritical members of the visible church who disobey Him. It is a distortion of the doctrine of eternal security to separate that truth from this equally valid truth: God demands godly living from all who profess to be His people. If we persist in sinning, we must face up to the consequences of such rebellion (Matt. 7:21-29).

PENITENCE

The word of the Lord that came to Joel, the son of Pethuel, is far more than a warning about impending punishment. It is also a clear call for us to exercise genuine penitence.

God's Call. God's call initially comes to the leaders of the people (Joel 1:13-14). The priests who serve at the altar, who minister in His holy presence, are called to put on sackcloth and mourn for the sins of the people. They must declare a holy fast and convene a sacred assembly. The elders are to be summoned to the house of God, that they may cry out to the Lord.

This same call then goes out to the people (1:15-20). As the threatened Day of the Lord draws near, the inhabitants of the land will become painfully aware that calamity is impending. In fact, the plants and the beasts of the field will be adversely affected because of the people's sins. Perhaps at the sight of parched vegetation and suffering livestock, Israel will be driven to make a fervent appeal to the only One who can help them.

God's Demand. When we sin, what exactly does God desire? Does He want some external act of penance, some formal gesture—such as the rending of one's garments or the keeping of a fast? (2:13, 15) Hardly. What God demands is an abstinence from all that displeases Him. He looks for far more than the outward ritual of tearing one's clothes to show sorrow and hatred for sin. His children must demonstrate a brokenness of heart and practice a confession and renunciation of sin. Not penance, but *penitence*—real, radical repentance—is what the Lord demands (2:12-17).

Martin Luther was keenly aware of the need for penitence in a believer's life. As he observed:

> To repent means to feel the wrath of God in earnest because of one's sin, so that the sinner experiences anguish of heart and is filled with a painful longing for the salvation and mercy of God. . . .Repentance is begun when we acknowledge our sins and are sincerely sorry for them; it is completed when trust in the mercy of God comes to this sorrow and hearts are converted to God, and long for the forgiveness of sins (Ewald Plass, ed., *What Luther Says*, Concordia, vol. 3, p. 1210).

God's Encouragement. Fortunately, the call to repentance which Joel announces is linked to the hope of God's mercy.

Without that hope, the penitent sinner would be little more than a prisoner trapped in the iron cage of despair. Those who are estranged are encouraged to come back to God, for He is merciful. Indeed, the Lord our God is:

> Gracious and compassionate,
> slow to anger and abounding in love,
> and He relents from sending calamity. . . .
> He may turn and have pity
> and leave behind a blessing (Joel 2:13-14).

This is just the sort of encouragement penitent sinners need. When the Spirit of God convicts us, and we realize our true condition, we can know that the Lord delights in mercy. As it is written:

> A bruised reed He will not break,
> and a smoldering wick He will not
> snuff out (Isa. 42:3).

Ask the Samaritan woman at Jacob's well in Sychar. Ask the dying thief at Calvary. Ask Simon Peter. Ask Saul of Tarsus. They will testify that God responded to their repentance with grace. Joel prophesies the good news that the forgiveness of sins can be found in God alone.

PROMISE
The third general theme of Joel's prophecy is that God promises a penitent people better times. They will abound in corn, wine, and oil. No longer will they be faced with drought, dust, dearth, and death. The Lord will restore to them the years that the locust had eaten (Joel 2:21-27).

However, when we obey God, we should look for blessings beyond those that He supplies through the world of nature. He offers us the great and wondrous blessings of His *grace*. The inestimable benefits of this gift are clearly promised to us in the words of Joel.

The Spirit. The first aspect of God's grace revealed in Joel concerns His guarantee that He will send us the Holy Spirit (2:28-29). This promise was fulfilled on that memorable feast of Pentecost, following the resurrection and ascension of our Lord (Acts 2:14-21). The Spirit was poured out on sons and daughters, patriarchs and servants. His arrival enabled believers to prophesy and see visions. The Spirit's presence in their lives gave them a clear perception of God's truth.

Yet to the unspiritual—the unregenerate—the things of God are dismissed as moronic (1 Cor. 2:14). These individuals cannot make sense of what the Bible says about sin, judgment, the need of regeneration, the value of the atonement, the pursuit of sanctification, or the return of Christ. The fact is, Satan—the god of this world—has blinded their minds and darkened their understanding to keep them from seeing the excellence of Christ and their desperate need of Him. Because of this, some of the world's greatest scientists and philosophers have failed to discover and appreciate the ultimate truth embodied in Christ.

When the Spirit comes, however, He enables the soul to see. We can have a knowledge of God through Jesus Christ (2 Cor. 4:3-6), and are empowered to communicate the Gospel to others in words of witness as well as deeds of love (John 14:16-17; 15:26; 16:13-14).

For many professing Christians, the Holy Spirit is still the forgotten person of the Trinity. They talk about Christ, and pray to the Father, but feel that the Spirit is preferred by sects on the fringe of repectable Christianity. But can we really know the Son who leads us to the Father, if the Spirit who introduces us to the Son does not lead us? While all believers do not have the gift of tongues (just as all Christians do not possess the gifts of healing, teaching, or administering), the Spirit indwells everyone who belongs to Christ and His body (1 Cor. 12:13). The Spirit regenerates us, illumines our minds, equips us to participate in God's family, sanctifies our personalities, conforms us to the likeness of Christ, and will raise us from the dust of death at the last day (John 3:3, 5; Rom. 8:9, 11, 14-17; 2 Thes. 2:13-14).

The Saviour. Even though the name of Jesus does not appear in the Book of Joel, the reality of salvation through Christ can be read between the lines of the Prophet's message (Joel 2:30-32). The outpouring of the Spirit not only will cause people to be aware of their sinful state, but will direct them to call on the name of the Lord for salvation. Out of the depths of their sin, oppressed by guilt and fear, they will appeal to Him who is able to save. He answers their cry, and sets them free from the penalty and power of sin (Rom. 10:11-13). All who sincerely turn to Christ for refuge from the condemnation and corruption of sin shall be saved. This is good news for sinful man.

It is interesting to note that Joel not only speaks of those who call on the name of the Lord, but also of the remnant whom the Lord calls (Joel 2:32). Is this a trivial play on words? Not at all. The remnant (termed "the survivors" in some translations), refers to the true people of God. These are believers who live among those who merely profess to serve the Lord. Many draw near to Him with their words, but their hearts are far from Him. Their names may be on church membership lists, but not necessarily in the Lamb's Book of Life. They seem satisfied with a superficial "churchianity," rather than a vital relationship with the living God. But when the winds of adversity sift through the visible church, the chaff is blown away and only the remnant remains.

The true people of God consist of all who call on the name of the Lord, renounce any belief in self-righteousness, and depend on Him alone for their salvation. Our calling on Him is the human side of the salvation experience; we must exercise repentance and faith. But His calling involves sovereign grace. The initiative belongs to Him. If we have responded to the Gospel, it is only because He first approached us and called us by name.

The Nations Judged. When God restores the fortunes of His people, Joel proclaims, He also will judge the nations that have mistreated them. He acts on behalf of Judah, Jerusalem, and Israel as He deals judicially with the pagan coastal towns of Tyre, Sidon, and Philistia (3:1-8).

Our deliverance from sin and oppression requires God's defeat of His enemies and ours. Christ liberates us from the power of the evil one and breaks the dominion of death. He goes forth, conquering and to conquer. As the Apostle John writes:

With justice He judges and makes war. His eyes are like

blazing fire, and on His head are many crowns. . . . He is
dressed in a robe dipped in blood, and His name is the
Word of God. . . . Out of His mouth comes a sharp sword
with which to strike down the nations. "He will rule them
with an iron scepter." He treads the winepress of the fury
of the wrath of God Almighty (Rev. 19:11-15).

A similar apocalyptic note is sounded in Joel. When God
roars from Zion and thunders from Jerusalem, earth and sky
will tremble. But His people will be secure in Him who is
their refuge and stronghold (Joel 3:14-16).

The People Blessed. The fourth promise mentioned in the
Book of Joel concerns future blessings (3:17-21). In overcoming the powers of evil and protecting His elect, the Lord God
will reveal Himself in all His glory and grace. He will dwell
in the midst of His people as a purifying presence and preserve them from every foe (3:17).

While Edom and Egypt will be made desolate in retribution
for the violence done to the people of Judah, the Lord's redeemed will know pardon and peace (3:18-21).

Joel's prophecy thus ends with a figurative description of
the blessings of the new age beyond the time of judgment. As
summarized by S.F. Winward:

Land and city alike are to be transformed. Judah will be
amazingly fertile, and life-giving waters will flow forth
from the Temple. Jerusalem, no longer violated by the heathen, will be the holy city, the dwelling place of God. Judah and Jerusalem, the land and the city, creation and community, the life of the countryside and the life of the town,
all that is of value in man's natural and social environment,
will be transformed and conserved in the new age (*A
Guide to the Prophets*, Hodder & Stoughton, p. 231).

The mystery of an unknown future is pictured in terms of
what we know now. Joel encourages us to believe that God
will bring about transformation, not obliteration, as the new
heaven and new earth become a glorious reality (Rev. 21:1).
And, most wonderful of all, the Lord will dwell in the midst
of His people forever (Joel 3:21; Rev. 21:2-4, 22-27; 22:1-5).

THREE

"The convictions of Amos were as different from those of his contemporaries as the convictions of Luther from those of the monks of his day" (M.S. and J.L. Miller, eds., HARPER'S BIBLE DICTIONARY, Harper & Brothers, p. 17).

"Amos was concerned to proclaim that a law broken through unrighteousness could not be mended by means of ritual, festival, or offering alone. . . . Righteousness was for Amos the most important moral attribute of the divine nature" (J.D. Douglas, ed., THE NEW BIBLE DICTIONARY, IVP, p. 33).

"Amos protested the perversion of justice . . . greedy oppression . . . luxurious living . . . sensual indulgence . . . ruthless exploitation of the weak" (H.E. Fosbroke, THE INTERPRETER'S BIBLE, Abingdon Press, P. 765).

"The prophet dwells on the irresistible, inescapable power of God only for the sake of enforcing demands growing out of his character. The attribute of justice or righteousness is especially prominent. Jehovah is represented as condemning injustice. . . . The total effect is to inspire awe and submission" (H.G. Mitchell, AMOS: AN ESSAY IN EXEGESIS, Bartlett, pp. 190, 193).

"To see in Amos only the denunciation of wrath and woe is to misunderstand the prophet." [He also proclaims blessing:] "The faithfulness of God to His covenant, and faithfulness which will be realized when God brings again the captivity of His people" (E.J. Young, AN INTRODUCTION TO THE OLD TESTAMENT, Eerdmans, p. 274).

AMOS
THE UNJUST
SOCIETY

MY FIRST PASTORATE was in the Italian Presbyterian Church of Montreal. While serving there, in addition to preaching, I also helped with the caretaking and other odd jobs. One Saturday morning, as I was hard at work repainting the church sign, a young French Canadian came along on his bicycle and struck up a conversation. As I continued lettering the sign, he asked all sorts of questions about the congregation's form of worship and government. He wondered about its views on priests, penance, purgatory, paradise, and the papacy.

As he prepared to resume his travels, he paused for a moment, then said: "For a sign painter, you know a lot about religion!"

Similarly, one might say of the shepherd Amos, "For a keeper of sheep, he knows a lot about theology!"

Amos came from Tekoa, a town twelve miles southeast of Bethlehem in Judea. Though a man of austerity and simplicity, God nonetheless called him to a meteoric ministry that may have lasted less than one week! "It seems certain," comments H.L. Ellison, "that his prophecy was given at the New Year festival at Bethel, probably spread over three days" (*The Old Testament Prophets*, Zondervan, p. 29).

Amos lived when Jeroboam II ruled in Israel (787-747 B.C.)

and Uzziah governed Judah (785-747 B.C.). His writing suggests that he was a rugged man, alert to the sights and sounds of his desolate land, aware of cause and effect in the natural world. His writings contain references to sunrises, eclipses, showers, tempests, stars, cedars, and oaks. Lions, sheep, birds, and snares also are mentioned. He sees men planting vineyards, treading grapes, and plowing fields. Importantly, he also perceives that external religion divorced from spiritual renewal and right relationships will lead inevitably and irrevocably to ruin.

Perhaps Amos' prophecy can best be understood, then, in light of the social, economic, political, and religious conditions of his time. Like Martin Luther at the Diet of Worms, Amos confronted the priest Amaziah and condemned Israel's adulterated worship. Chafing under this the prophet's all too accurate charges, Amaziah falsely accused Amos of sedition in an attempt to silence him (Amos 7:10-17). But the shepherd whom God had called to speak His Word refused to be intimidated.

We need to hear the prophetic voice of that brave man in our own time, since the faults and dangers of which he warned are still with us. An outline of this book appears as follows:

(1) **Denouncing Sin**
   A. The Nations (1:3—2:3)
   B. The Israelites (2:4-8)

(2) **Pronouncing Sentence**
   A. Indictment (3:1—4:1; 6:12-14; 5:10, 12; 6:1-6; 5:11-12; 8:5-6; 5:5; 8:14)
   B. Impenitence (4:6-13)
   C. Punishment (7:7-9; 1:4-5, 7-8, 10, 12, 14-15; 2:2-3, 9—3:2)
   D. Pain (5:1-3, 21-24)

(3) **Announcing Salvation**
   A. Promise of Life (5:4-6, 14-15)
   B. Promise of Restoration (5:15; 9:11-15)

Denouncing Sin

Amos speaks for God with brutal frankness. There is no ambiguity whatsoever in his description and denunciation of sin. Unlike cowards who seek a way of evasion, compromise, or capitulation when faced with a difficult task, Amos courageously exposes the moral evils existing in his society. "He represents that challenge to established form and order which has repeatedly been necessary to free the church from the tyranny of tradition," H.L. Ellison notes (*The Old Testament Prophets,* Zondervan, p. 29).

The Nations. Amos begins his denunciation by exposing and condemning the sins of the nations. He speaks for the Judge of all the earth, and points to particular acts and attitudes that call for judgment:

● Damascus is guilty of cruelty and violence against Gilead. The royal house shall be devastated by fire, and its fortresses destroyed. The dwellers in the Valley of Aven ("the vale of wickedness") shall not escape. Exile awaits these aggressors (Amos 1:3-5).
● Gaza has merited God's wrath because it is guilty of having carried away captives (1:6-8).
● Tyre the treacherous has sold whole communities of captives to Edom, thus breaking a treaty of brotherhood (1:9-10).
● Edom, with its stifling of compassion and violence against a related people, shall feel God's wrath (1:11-12).
● Ammon, whose people have ripped open the pregnant women of Gilead, shall encounter the Lord's fury (1:13-15).
● Moab, infamous for having burned the king of Edom's bones into lime to be used as mortar, shall be exposed to death and destruction (2:1-3).

The Israelites. Having denounced the sins of the heathen nations, Amos probably won a round of applause from the people of Israel. But now he turns to Judah and Israel and condemns *their* sins as well.

● Judah has rejected the law of the Lord, disobeyed His decrees, followed false gods, and so deserves God's wrath (2:4-5).

• Israel has notoriously exploited the poor and oppressed the defenseless (2:6-8). It is guilty of denying justice to those who have been victimized, and of tolerating incest. The nation has given itself over to "luxury, oppression, perversion of justice, cruelty, profaneness, unreal service, and real apostasy" (E.B. Pusey, *The Minor Prophets*, Walter Smith/Mozely, pp. 173-174).

Does it surprise us to find Judah and Israel listed among those nations whose sins are denounced? Are they not God's covenant people, the chosen ones to whom the Lord has given great privileges and glowing promises? Will not the Lord overlook their transgressions?

Unfortunately, though they once were united under the rule of Saul, David, and Solomon, they now are at odds with each other and with God. The Divided Kingdom is depraved in both its parts and will not be spared when the Almighty reveals His wrath against the unrighteousness of men.

Pronouncing Sentence

Indictment. The word of the Lord is directed to both the Northern Kingdom of Israel and the Southern Kingdom of Judah—against the whole family that was brought up out of Egypt (Amos 3:1). Though His people have been endowed with many blessings, they still will be punished for their sins (3:2).

As mentioned earlier, Amos is aware of cause and effect relationships. He realizes, therefore, that when people sin, the consequence is judgment (3:3-6). The Lord will allow the heathen to overrun the land as punishment for Israel's sin (3:7-15).

There is nothing vague about the charges God's spokesman makes in his indictment against the covenant people. He cites such wrongs as:

• The extravagance of the rich who have mansions, summer houses, and winter houses, but who are insensitive to the needs of the homeless (3:15).
• The self-indulgence of intemperate and gluttonous women, whose insatiable appetites push their husbands to earn

more—even if it means oppressing the poor and crushing the needy (4:1).

• The perversion of justice, through bribery and intimidation, aggravating the plight of the widow, the orphan, and the poor (6:12-14; 5:10, 12).

• The complacency of Zion (Judah, the Southern Kingdom) and Mount Samaria (Israel, the Northern Kingdom), which indulge themselves in a most extravagant lifestyle while others suffer hunger and thirst on the edge of society (6:1-6).

• The amassing of fortunes by force and fraud; climbing to the top on the backs of the exploited poor (5:11-12).

• The advancement of business through the use of false weights and measures, cheating the consumer, and encroaching on the day set apart for rest and worship (8:5).

• The enslavement of persons who are considered worth less than things (8:6).

• The worship of false gods and the adulteration of the worship of the true God at shrines such as those located at Gilgal, Bethel, Dan, and Beersheba (5:5; 8:14).

This is, to say the least, quite a list.

Impenitence. Not only has God warned the Israelites of coming judgment, but He has chastised them to humble their pride and to rescue them from the way that leads to death. Yet Israel's behavior has not changed.

He sent them hunger, for example, yet they did not return to Him (4:6). In the course of His providence, the Lord withheld the rain from them. Yet drought did not drive them back to God (4:7-8). Blight and mildew struck the vineyards. Locusts devoured their fig and olive trees. Still Israel persisted in turning away from God (4:9). Plagues came upon them, but they resisted the call of Him who holds the secret of wholeness in His hands (4:10). The calamities that devastated them did not break their stubborn wills (4:11). Therefore, Amos claims, let Israel prepare to meet the Lord God Almighty and face His judgment (4:12-13).

Punishment. Many Christians have become so afraid of being labeled "judgmental," that they let grave injustices pass without open criticism. They may even try to justify their silence by referring to the words of Jesus: "Do not judge, or you too will be judged. For in the same ways you judge others, you will be judged, and with the measure you use, it will be measured to you" (Matt. 7:1-2). But such an interpretation would inevitably have us doing away with our judicial systems and the concept of church discipline. Granted, our Lord *does* warn us against having a harsh, censorious, fault-finding attitude—the sort of disposition ready to condemn in others what we are willing to excuse in ourselves. But He is not teaching us to be indifferent to moral evil.

When Amos denounces sin and pronounces sentence, he is expressing God's repugnance toward sin. As a builder uses a plumb line to determine if his work is straight, so the Lord measures and evaluates the conduct of His people. God's authoritative standard tells us what is acceptable or unacceptable in His eyes. We are not free to commend or condone what God condemns in Holy Scripture (Amos 7:7-9).

Weighed in God's balances and found wanting, measured by His standard and exposed as deviant, Damascus, Gaza, Tyre, Edom, Ammon, and Moab will feel the full impact of God's judgment. Neither massive walls, opulent palaces, nor powerful princes shall be spared in that dread day (1:4-5, 7-8, 10, 12, 14-15; 2:2-3).

Israel and Judah, like their pagan neighbors, also will be sentenced on account of their sins. Their guilt is greater than that of the heathen, for they have sinned while knowing exactly what God required of them. The Lord provided Israel with special revelations, set them free from the slavery of Egypt, defeated the Amorites on their behalf, and sent them prophets to make known His truth (2:9-11). He has shown His love to Israel and Judah in a unique way, entering into a covenant relationship with them. Yet they have gone after the idols and ideologies of the pagan world. Is it any wonder that the Lord now vows to punish them for all their sins? (2:12—3:2)

Pain. God's heart is hurt by the ingratitude and insolence of those who follow a death-style destined to end in misery. He takes up a lament for Israel and pours out His grief (5:1-3) for He knows that what now appears to be an affluent society shall soon be reduced to ruins.

All this is not to say that Israel had no religion. This nation was *very* religious. Shrines, altars, rituals, ceremonies, priests, sacrifices—all these elements were very much in evidence. But the people wrongly imagined that they could manipulate God by doing "the rite thing." They assumed He would be satisfied with the performance of externally impressive rituals, and failed to understand that the Lord really desired obedience and justice. Corrupt worship only displeased the Lord and aggravated the people's guilt:

> I hate, I despise your religious feasts; I cannot stand your assemblies. Even though you bring Me burnt offerings and grain offerings, I will not accept them. . . .Away with the noise of your songs! I will not listen to the music of your harps. But let justice roll on like a river, righteousness like a never-failing stream! (5:21-24)

Beyond all doubt,

> Such worship is a profane travesty, for it was the act of men and women morally unclean and unwilling to submit to the searching discipline of God. . . . Religion had become externalized and materialized. The prophet will have it internalized and moralized. . . . He will not accept a religion that excludes morality (John Paterson, *The Goodly Fellowship of the Prophets*, Charles Scribner's Sons, p. 25).

Do we see the relevance of the message of Amos to our contemporary situation? Like Judah and Israel, the church today has spiritual privileges. They had circumcision and the Passover. We have baptism and the Lord's Supper. They had the Law and the Prophets. We have even more—the fullness of revelation in Christ and the witness of the apostles.

Like Judah and Israel, we may think that performing religious rituals on the Sabbath is sufficient to satisfy God's requirements; yet we then live our lives the other six days of the week as though He did not matter. We can say the Lord's Prayer, recite the Apostles' Creed, outline the plan of salvation, and pay our tithe—and *still* be guilty of dishonesty in business, insensitivity to the poor, and immorality in the expression of our God-given sexuality.

Such folly is fatal to those who commit it, and it brings grief to God. What God demands is nothing less than a double conversion. First, we must turn from sin to Him who offers new life. Then, we must turn to our neighbor and deal with him justly. Ritual observance without the practice of righteousness is not acceptable in God's sight.

This strong emphasis on demonstrating a right relationship with God by practicing justice is a major theme in the prophecy of Amos. We should bear in mind that biblical prophecy is no mere lyrical outpouring abounding in simile and metaphor, designed to warm our emotions and stimulate the imagination for a fleeting moment. No, God's prophetic word is meant to change our lifestyles for good. Scripture not only tells us how we may be saved, but calls on us to seek justice in th social order.

The prophets tell us to get right with God. That vertical relationship is of absolute importance and must be restored; there can be no new life without it. But the prophets also make it abundantly clear that our horizontal relationships with men on earth validate the authenticity of our professed relationship to God in heaven.

We certainly should be concerned with spreading the Gospel and deepening our commitment to Christ as we grow in our Christian walk. But we also should seriously seek to transform social structures that permit and even perpetuate racism and poverty. With this holistic approach to life, God is well pleased.

ANNOUNCING SALVATION

The Lord who denounces sin and pronounces sentence also announces salvation through his servant, Amos. He brings us a promise of life and restoration.

Promise of Life. This is God's word to His people:

> Seek Me and live; do not seek Bethel, do not go to Gilgal, do not journey to Beersheba. For Gilgal will surely go into exile, and Bethel will be reduced to nothing. Seek the Lord and live (5:4-6).

Don't look to idol shrines and impotent ideologies for help, Amos is saying. Seek the living God, and Him alone, to discover and experience true life.

Instead of perverting justice and oppressing the helpless,

Seek good, not evil, that you may live. Then the Lord God Almighty will be with you, just as you say He is. Hate evil, love good; maintain justice in the courts. Perhaps the Lord God Almighty will have mercy on the remnant of Joseph (5:14-15).

Through God's mercy a remnant, a group of survivors in the Northern Kingdom, will be allowed to exist. Therefore, let those who claim to be the Lord's own people demonstrate their identity by pursuing what is morally excellent. They must make a radical break with what He declares to be morally evil.

Promise of Restoration. Amos affirms that God's offer of life is not limited to the people of Judah and Israel, but extends even to the pagan peoples of the earth. The remnant (5:15) shall be greatly enlarged when God fulfills His promise of restoration. He says:

In that day I will restore David's fallen tent. I will repair its broken places, restore its ruins, and build it as it used to be, so that they may possess the remnant of Edom and all the nations that bear My name (9:11-12).

What the Lord promises, He will surely perform. David's royal house shall be repaired and restored from its fallen condition. In his commentary on this passage, Theodore Laetsch observes:

The restored house of David will not be a house divided against itself, engaged in internecine strife. There will be one King and one kingdom (Ezek. 37:22) .... Restored to strength and beauty, it will stand before all the world, a holy temple of God (1 Cor. 3:17; Eph. 2:20-22; 5:27; Rev. 21:2-4). Not only will it regain all its glory as in the days of old (compare 1 Kings 10:4-9), it will extend to the end of the world, as prophesied by Psalms 22:27-28; 45:3-6; 72:7-11; 89:14-37 (*The Minor Prophets*, Concordia, p. 191).

The fulfillment of this promise already is a reality. When the Jerusalem Council met to discuss matters concerning the nature and mission of the church, James, the brother of our Lord, referred to the promise of restoration mentioned in Amos (Acts 15:13-18). At the time, the apostles were debating the status of Gentile converts to Christianity. Should they be welcomed into the fellowship of congregations consisting mainly of Jewish Christians after submitting to circumcision? Or was faith in Jesus as the Messiah sufficient to qualify them for membership in the messianic community? The Council opted for the latter view, on the basis of the quotation from the prophecy of Amos.

Jews and Gentiles who accept Jesus as the Christ thus have equal standing in the one family of God. David's fallen house is built up, repaired, and restored, as converts come into God's kingdom (Eph. 2:11-12).

The glowing vision that concludes the prophecy of Amos is luminous with prosperity and security for the people of God. The land will yield a superabundant harvest, and returning exiles will rebuild what had been ruined (Amos 9:13-15). Surely, the future is as bright as the promises of God!

FOUR

"Obadiah, the shortest book of the Old Testament, is marked by a vigorous poetic language. . . . Various striking comparisons and metaphors are used. . . . Obadiah proceeds from the particular to the general, from the judgment of Edom to universal judgment, from the restoration of Israel to the establishment of the kingdom of God" (J.D. Douglas, ed., THE NEW BIBLE DICTIONARY, IVP, p. 903).

"The book is a fiery denunciation of Judah's traditional enemies . . . an historic situation gives way to Apocalyptic prophecies of deeds and dreams that will be brought to fruition in the reign of the Lord" (M.S. and J.L. Miller, eds., HARPER'S BIBLE DICTIONARY, Harper & Brothers, p. 499).

"The kingdom of our Lord and Saviour Jesus Christ . . . is not to be confused or identified with any temporal dominion exercised by earthly powers. Scripture points on beyond all our conflicts, all our revolutions, all our wars, to the kingdom where God reigns by the power of grace" (G.A. Buttrick, ed., THE INTERPRETER'S BIBLE, Abingdon Press, vol. 6, p. 867).

"Though Obadiah may seem preoccupied with the restoration of Israel, the closing words of the prophecy show that he knew all this was to come to pass merely that the kingdom of God should be established" (H.L. Ellison, THE PROPHETS OF ISRAEL, Eerdmans, p. 97).

OBADIAH
THE BOTTOM
LINE

MARY WAS BORN IN SCOTLAND during that decade of the nineteenth century known as "the hungry forties." Unemployment raged in the cities, crop failure plagued the countryside, and misery reigned everywhere. Some people turned to begging and others to stealing in the struggle for survival. Mary's mother was a weaver, but an alcoholic father squandered her hard-earned money. At the age of eleven, Mary went to work in the mills. Her father's condition worsened and the family pawned its belongings to meet basic expenses. But young Mary's mother had faith in the living God and she encouraged her daughter to follow Christ.

At church one evening, Mary was fascinated by the reports she heard from a missionary serving in Africa. Soon thereafter, she began to read her New Testament. She also learned about the career of David Livingstone. By teaching Sunday School, leading a youth group, and growing in her knowledge of the Lord, Mary prepared for service in what now is Nigeria.

Swamps, insects, fever, witchcraft, ritual murder, and tribal wars greeted her in Africa. But by founding an orphanage, teaching children, nursing the sick, and settling feuds, she pointed people to Christ. Her service was sustained by persevering prayer and the promises of God in Scripture. She had an unwavering faith in the reality and sovereignty of God.

Mary Slessor of Calabar apparently agreed with Obadiah the prophet, who was convinced that the Lord's kingship would ultimately be universally acknowledged. That knowledge spurred her on.

But who in the world is this Obadiah? The Bible gives us no data with which to construct a definitive biography of him, much less "market" him as a religious celebrity. Yet it is clear that Obadiah was a man to whom God gave a vision, a man whose priority was to deliver with total fidelity whatever the sovereign Lord said. Obadiah was a servant of the One who shatters the silence and reveals His will.

The main emphases of this brief but potent prophecy may be outlined as follows:

(1) Divine Severity
   A. Edom Denounced (1-9)
   B. Judgment Deserved (10-14)
   C. Nations Defeated (15-16)

(2) Divine Sovereignty
   Triumph of the King (17-21)

DIVINE SEVERITY

Edom Denounced. Obadiah's message from the Lord is directed against Edom and expresses the severity of God's justice in no uncertain terms.

The Edomites were descendants of Esau the profane, who bartered away his birthright for a bowl of red stew (Gen. 25:30). They occupied a wilderness region that stretched from the edge of the Dead Sea to the shores of the Red Sea (Josh. 15:1). The mountainous land of Edom included towns such as Bozrah, Teman, Sela, and Petra. Tourists still marvel at the monumental remains of Petra, magnificently carved in pink stone.

Originally ruled by tribal chiefs, the Edomites later were governed by kings (Gen. 36:31-39). But Obadiah predicts that the proud inhabitants of Edom are doomed to destruction (vv. 1-9). Dwelling in the clefts of the rocks, smugly satisfied, feeling secure from all attack, the Edomites will find that their impregnable fortress is vulnerable. Exalted as the eagle, looking down on the rest of the world haughtily from the heights, setting their nest among the stars, the proud people of Edom shall be humiliated in the dust. Their own allies will become their foes and prevail against them. Contemptuous hearts, conceited attitudes, vaunted wisdom—all these shall be exposed as folly and end in slaughter.

Judgment Deserved. What has motivated this devastating judgment of God against the Edomites? Why should they be struck with destruction and dismay? First, it is important to remember that the revelation of God's wrath is never the expression of irrational rage. Our God is no capricious pagan divinity, wreaking havoc indiscriminately on humanity. Accordingly, Obadiah clearly states the reasons for God's wrath.

Not only does Edom deserve to be punished for its pride, he says, but it also draws down wrath for the cruelty it has shown Judah during times of crisis (10-14).

We know that when the people of Israel requested permission to pass through Edom after the Exodus, the Edomites denied it to them (Num. 20:14-21). When Pekah and Rezin attacked Judah, the Edomites also invaded and carried away captives (2 Chron. 28:17). Likewise, they rejoiced over the fall of Judah (Ps. 137:7), watched the defilement of Jerusalem by the heathen, participated in the sacrilegious plunder, and when some of the people of Judah tried to flee their oppressor, Edom actually blocked their route of escape. In short, in the day of Judah's distress, Edom gloated with glee.

Is it any wonder, then, that the Lord God vows to reward such malice and violence with the revelation of His wrath?

Nations Defeated. The Day of the Lord—the manifestation of His justice on man's inhumanity to man—is about to dawn. Obadiah, like Jeremiah (Jer. 49:7-22) and Ezekiel (Ezek. 25:12-14), prophesies the defeat of the proud (Obad. 15-16). Crimes committed with impunity have not escaped God's all-seeing eyes. Iniquity shall receive retribution at the hands of Him who is perfect in holiness and righteousness. No one can fool God. As men and nations sow, so shall they eventually reap. Unless Edom demonstrates radical repentance, irreparable ruin is inevitable. Violence will be answered by the apocalypse of divine vengeance and malice by the manifestation of His might. The Day of the Lord shall surely dawn, and His purifying indignation burn.

True to Obadiah's word, the Edomites eventually were conquered by the Chaldeans in the sixth century B.C., and by the
Nabateans in the third century B.C. The lesson here should be
clear: no nation is exempt from God's government. What He
seemingly ignores during our lifetime will surely be subject to
His judgment at the last day. As Calvin comments:

> The Lord hastens not after the manner of men; but at the
> same time, He knows His own seasons; and this is ever
> accomplished, that when the ungodly think themselves to
> be at rest, then sudden destruction overtakes them. . . . As
> God has proved Himself to be One who justly punishes
> sins with respect to Israel and Judah, so also at length He
> will ascend His tribunal to judge all the nations. . . . All in
> their different conditions shall be constrained to give an
> account of their actions, for the Lord will spare none (John
> Calvin, *Commentaries on the Minor Prophets*, Calvin
> Translation Society, vol. 2, pp. 445-446).

The marvels of human progress have often been celebrated
in our century. Expositions and world's fairs have been held
in great cities like New York, Paris, Montreal, and Seattle. We
have been amazed at the achievements of science and tech-
nology, and found fresh ideas about the conquest of disease,
poverty, racism, hunger, and war.

Yet the twentieth century also has witnessed economic oppression, political dictatorship, totalitarian aggression, religious persecution, environmental pollution, and racial discrimination on an unprecedented scale. The true and living
God is neither deaf nor blind to these crimes. He sees violence and hears the victim's cry. He is not insensitive to the
deplorable suffering caused by man's inhumanity to man.
Whether in the course of our years, or at the final judgment,
God *will* bring the Edomites of every generation down from
their rest among the stars to the dust of death.

DIVINE SOVEREIGNTY

Triumph of the King. Edom's doom also will be Jacob's deliverance, Obadiah announces (17-21). This will certainly come

to pass, because the Lord has declared it and He cannot lie. Unlike some persuasive demagogues who are long on promises before elections and short on performance afterward, God keeps His word. If He promises to punish evil and save His people, you can rely on Him to fulfill both warning and promise. God does not wilt nor waver. His will certainly shall find fulfillment, "and the kingdom will be the Lord's" (v. 21).

Our security, then, is bound up with God's sovereignty. The final word rests not with Pharaoh, but with the Lord who defeated him and delivered Israel. The final outcome is not in the hands of the Babylonians who carried the Jews away into captivity, but in Him who raised up Cyrus as His instrument of liberation. Nero, Domitian, Diocletian—all of these Roman emperors struggled against the church. Yet they have passed from the scene, while the church endures and grows through the passing centuries. Marx, Lenin, Stalin, Mao, Hitler, Mussolini—they are dead and buried. Yet the King of kings lives and reigns because of the good pleasure of Him who works all things after the counsel of His will (Eph. 1:11).

We can see the destiny of God's kingdom in the experience of Christ the King. The nations raged furiously together, their leaders conspired against Him, they treated Him with contempt and nailed Him to a cross. But God has willed that His royal Son should rule on Zion's hill. He has resolved to give Him the peoples of the earth as His inheritance. And so it shall come to pass, regardless of rejection and revolution on the part of the reprobate (Ps. 2:1-12). The crucified Christ is now crowned with glory and honor (Heb. 2:7). All authority and power, in heaven and on earth, belong to Him (Matt. 28:18; Phil. 2:6-11).

In the end, God's authority will be vindicated and His power manifested. Not even the gates of hell shall prevail to prevent the fulfillment of the King's plan. Then we will hear the shout of triumph:

The kingdom of this world has become the kingdom of our Lord and of His Christ, and He will reign for ever and ever (Rev. 11:15).

Hallelujah! Salvation and glory and power belong to our God, for true and just are His judgments.... Hallelujah! For our Lord God Almighty reigns. Let us rejoice and be glad and give Him glory! (19:1-7).

Obadiah's prophecy is thus far more than "a burning, scorching, blasting book ... a hymn of hate ... a fiery cry of hatred" expressing "the rage of a brother betrayed" (John Paterson, *The Goodly Fellowship of the Prophets*, Charles Scribner's Sons, pp. 184-185). It is a magnificent affirmation of God's greatness, holiness, and righteousness. The kingdom belongs universally and everlastingly to Him alone.

But one question remains: namely, is there no hope for the Edomites? Are they doomed to destruction? Actually, Obadiah's stern sentence of doom is not the final word on their fate. His prophecy closes with a glorious promise:

By the gracious power of God, who grants a return even to captives in distant countries, there is deliverance also for Edom! God's liberated people, grateful for their own safety, will "ascend Mount Zion and proclaim salvation to Edom, their enemy and oppressor.... Salvation for the Gentiles comes from no other source than the salvation of the Jews, from Zion, where God has revealed Himself as the God of grace, from the Jews, of whom as concerning the flesh Christ came.... Jehovah is the Lord of unfathomable grace (Theodore Laetsch, *The Minor Prophets*, Concordia, pp. 212-213).

Thus, deliverers or proclaimers of the Good News will go up on Mount Zion and bring blessing to the inhabitants of the mountains of Esau (Obad. 21). So shall the kingdom be the Lord's.

Community of the King? We can rejoice in the truth of Obadiah's bottom line—that the kingdom is God's—and praise Him who is King over all. But that is not enough. Christians must live as the community of the King in a world dominated by the prince of darkness. Here and now, we are called to radical discipleship and fervent witness. We are to live as those who anticipate the full revelation of His glorious victory, following the ethical standards found in Scripture rather than the guidelines of this evil age.

This will require our total commitment, something quite different from mere tokenism or superficial believism. Some profess allegiance to the King, but their lifestyle is as materialistic as that of any secular humanist—except that they cover it over with a "Jesus veneer."

Calvin reminds us of the difference which God's sole kingship should make in our lives:

When God does not appear as the only King, all things are in confusion, without any order. Now God is not called a King by way of an empty distinction. Then only is He regarded a King in reality, when all submit themselves to Him, when they are ruled by His Word; in short, when all creatures become silent in His presence (*Commentaries on the Minor Prophets*, vol. 2, p. 455).

Obadiah would surely have agreed with such a sentiment.

FIVE

"In narrating his own experience in the matter of his commission to Ninevah, Jonah intended to teach his people the lesson of the inclusiveness of the Divine government, and thus to rebuke the exclusiveness of their attitude to surrounding peoples" (G. Campbell Morgan, THE ANALYZED BIBLE, F.H. Revell, p. 301).

"The primary message of the book is clearly that God's interest and mercy extend far beyond the Jews to the whole human race" (J.D. Douglas, ed., THE NEW BIBLE DICTIONARY, IVP, p. 653).

"The fundamental purpose of the book . . . is not found in its missionary or universalistic teaching. It is rather to show that Jonah being cast into the depths of Sheol and yet brought up alive is an illustration of the death of the Messiah for sins not His own and of the Messiah's resurrection" (E.J. Young, AN INTRODUCTION TO THE OLD TESTAMENT, Eerdmans, p. 280).

"Our Lord accepted the events here narrated as historical. This is important for us who believe in Him as our precious Saviour, the Son of the Father, faultless in His humanity. And perhaps it may mean something to those who share this belief, but do not fully and entirely agree with us in accepting the Old Testament as an integral part of the infallible, authoritative Word of God" (G.C. Aalders, THE PROBLEM OF THE BOOK OF JONAH, Tyndale, pp. 29-30).

JONAH THE RELUCTANT MISSIONARY

WHAT KEEPS US FROM OBEYING our Lord's Great Commission? Are we afraid to confront today's secular humanism with a Gospel that comes from the distant past? Perhaps we're reluctant to share our faith because we're not exactly sure *how* to lead others to Christ. Maybe we're simply convinced that any mention of the Word should be confined to Sunday morning, limited to church property, and left exclusively to an ordained minister.

The Book of Jonah tells of yet another great menace to the spread of the Gospel: a narrow, sectarian nationalism that looks at the rest of the world with contempt rather than compassion. We'll deal with this theme throughout this chapter. But first, let's look at what some commentators have termed "the problem of Jonah."

Simply stated, some people find the story of Jonah and the great fish hard to swallow. They theorize that a ship named *Whale* rescued the wayward prophet as he floundered on the high seas. What we have here, then, is an allegory with a moral—but certainly not a historical account.

Zealous defenders of the faith, on the other hand, have turned the Book of Jonah into a battleground for zoological debate. Speculating about the size of fishes and the possibility of survival within a marine monster, they have helped put

Jonah's story in the category of "believe it or not" tales.

Our Lord's own statements, however, assume the historicity of Jonah; in fact, He uses the events narrated in this prophet's book to point to His own death and resurrection (Matt. 12:40-41).

Let us therefore consider the message of this book as true, and view it in terms of five interrelated themes: commission, contradiction, confession, conversion, and compassion:

(1) Commission
   A. From the Lord (1:1)
   B. To the City (1:2)

(2) Contradiction
   A. Evasion (1:3-8)
   B. Exposure (1:9-17)

(3) Confession
   A. Danger (2:1-6)
   B. Deliverance (2:6-10)

(4) Conversion
   A. Proclamation (3:1-4)
   B. Response (3:5-9)
   C. Forgiveness (3:10)

(5) Compassion
   A. Complaint (4:1-3)
   B. Correction (4:4)
   C. Renewed Complaint (4:5-9)
   D. Renewed Correction (4:10)

COMMISSION

Concerning the commission of Jonah, the son of Amittai (2 Kings 14:25), we need to notice that his instructions came from the Lord and that he was directed to preach to the city of Nineveh.

From the Lord. Jonah was a man to whom "the word of the Lord came" (1:1). The God of the Bible is not a deaf, dumb, or dead nonentity. He speaks. His word is dynamic, moving from

His heart and mind to ours. Sometimes the living God speaks in accents of grace, giving us promises of forgiveness and new life. At other times the Lord addresses us with authority, proposing precepts for our obedience. In Jonah's case, elements of both of these imperatives were evident.

To the City. What did the Lord tell Jonah? "Go to the great city of Nineveh and preach against it, because its wickedness has come up before Me" (1:2).

Situated on a plain along the left bank of the Tigris, Nineveh, the capital of the Assyrian kingdom, was surrounded by walls that rose to a height of 100 feet; they were so thick that three chariots could run abreast at the top. The Assyrian people were noted for their engineering expertise, aggressive attitude, and military might. They also were notorious for their cruelty to captives.

God saw the wickedness of the people of Nineveh and was not indifferent to their injustice, intemperance, immorality, and idolatry. The holy Lord, in His righteousness, weighed the people and found them sorely wanting. So He commissioned Jonah to go and declare that the wrath of God was about to be revealed against the unrighteousness of these men.

The Jehovah who sent Jonah to Nineveh also sends the church into the world with His Word of law and grace. The Lord Jesus declares, "As the Father has sent Me, I am sending you" (John 20:21).

CONTRADICTION

Instead of complying with the Lord's commission, Jonah took the route of evasion. Yet he eventually was exposed as a fugitive from God.

Evasion. Jonah, like many in the church today, disobeyed his divine commission. Instead of going to Nineveh, he went to the seaport city of Joppa (modern Jaffa) and found a ship headed in the opposite direction—to Tarshish. Jonah paid his fare, boarded the boat, and thus sought to run from the presence of the Lord (Jonah 1:3-8).

Jonah's desertion was not merely a matter of geography. Rather, it involved his decision to choose *his* will over God's.

Anyone who refuses to fulfill the Lord's orders joins Jonah in buying a ticket to Tarshish. God commands civil authorities to restrain evil in society and to protect the lives of law-abiding citizens. But if rulers yield to bribery or intimidation, or fail to enforce justice in the social order, they are on their way to Tarshish. Likewise, God calls employers to give their workers a fair wage, and workers to do their appointed tasks with competence and honesty. The refusal to do this is nothing less than disobedience and desertion. Parents are commanded to bring up their children in the ways of the Lord, by prayer, precept, and personal example. Dereliction puts such delinquent parents on board ship with Jonah, bound for Tarshish.

Now contrast these examples with the attitude of Samuel, who said: "Speak, Lord, for Your servant is listening" (1 Sam. 3:9), or that of Isaiah: "Here am I. Send me!" (Isa. 6:8) This is the type of obedience that will keep us off ships which are sailing away from God.

Exposure. When Jonah contradicted God's commission instead of complying with it, the Lord sent a great wind on the sea, and a violent storm threatened to break up the ship. Terrified, the sailors cried out to whatever gods they remembered. They threw the cargo into the sea to lighten the ship and keep it afloat. Then the captain went below deck, roused the fugitive prophet from his sleep, and asked him to pray for safety through this fearful calamity.

Eventually, the sailors cast lots in an effort to determine who was responsible for the storm that involved them all. The lot fell to Jonah. Under questioning, he was forced to admit that he was a Hebrew, a worshiper of the Lord—the God of heaven, maker of land and sea, the One from whom escape was utterly impossible.

Can you imagine how ashamed Jonah felt when pagan, idolatrous sailors revealed his disobedience? Isn't it similarly dreadful when the secular world is able to point out the scandalous inconsistencies of a church that professes one thing, but practices another?

Jonah acknowledged his guilt, and told the mariners that calm would return only if his sin was punished. Not wanting to put Jonah to death, they tried rowing to shore, to deposit the fugitive prophet there; they were frustrated in this effort. Finally, in desperation, they cast Jonah into the sea; immediately, the roaring winds and raging waves grew peaceful (1:15).

In tempestuous sixteenth-century England, Bishop John Hooper of Gloucester applied this passage to the state of his nation. He observed that every ruler and every judge should learn to "cast out of their commonwealth as many Jonases as they find stubborn, and will not amend their lives" (John Hooper, *The Early Writings*, Parker Society, pp. 480-481).

CONFESSION

The same Lord who sent the storm also "provided a great fish to swallow Jonah, and Jonah was inside the fish three days and three nights" (Jonah 1:17).

As Jonah had confessed his faith and his fault to the sailors on board ship, so now entombed within a whale, he confesses danger and celebrates his deliverance.

Danger. From inside the great fish, the runaway prophet prays to the Lord his God (2:1-6). From the depths of destruction, from the very abyss of death, Jonah prays. Out of the depths, in dire distress, he cries for help. As the currents swirl about him, while waves and breakers sweep over him, with seaweed wrapped around his head, sinking downward to the roots of the mountains, Jonah cries to the Lord with a sense of urgency. Whereas on land he fled to sea that he might *evade* God's presence, Jonah now earnestly *seeks* the Lord. A deep sense of need often works wonders in moving us from the mere formality of prayer to fervent pleading before God!

Deliverance. Drawing on the language of remembered psalms, Jonah thinks of the power and goodness of God (2:6-10). From the deep heart of the seas, he cries out to the heart of God. Confident of the Lord's mercy and might, he gives thanks to the God of salvation. The Lord will bring Jonah's life up from the grave. At the Lord's command, the great fish will disgorge Jonah onto dry land.

Many Bible students wonder whether the Lord's miraculous intervention actually kept Jonah alive. I believe so. After all, if God can keep an unborn child alive for nine months in its mother's womb, surely He can sustain a mature man inside a marine monster for three days. Did Jonah actually experience death, followed by resurrection? This too is a possibility with

Him, who is the Lord of life.

But *why* did the Lord deliver Jonah from the danger of death? Several reasons may be suggested:

• To show God's mercy to sinners who confess their faults with real repentance. If the Lord has been gracious to a rebellious prophet, will He not be merciful to us when we approach Him with humble, contrite hearts?

• To give Jonah another opportunity to complete his God-given assignment in Nineveh. When we fail to fulfill our vocation, let us trust in the goodness of God who grants us the privilege of beginning again.

• To point forward to Christ. Here we see a witness to Jesus' death and resurrection. Our Lord refers to the story of Jonah on at least two occasions, but in neither case does He suggest that it is an allegory or a parable (Matt. 12:40-41; Luke 11:29-32). The Messiah interprets the story as history with a significance beyond itself: It foretells His own rising from the dead on the third day after His redemptive death at the cross.

CONVERSION

Proclamation. Jonah's stubborn streak is more than matched by the persistent patience of the Lord. God's word comes to Jonah a second time:

> Go to the great city of Nineveh and proclaim to it the message I give you (Jonah 3:1-2).

For the disobedient and impenitent, there will be no second chance beyond this world—only that "second death" from which there can be no resurrection to everlasting blessedness (John 8:24; Rev. 20:6, 14). But here and now, in this day of grace, the word of the Lord may come to us "a second time."

Simon Peter, like Jonah, heard the word of the Lord "a second time." After his shameful denial of the Master, he wept bitterly. But the risen Christ met him, drew from him a threefold affirmation of love as if to cancel out that threefold denial, and renewed Peter's commission to shepherd His flock (John 21:15-17).

God's commission is unchanging. Jonah is to go where the Lord sends him. He must deliver the message God gives him. The servant of the Word is under orders. He has a sacred obligation to speak what he has heard from the mouth of the Lord, without addition, subtraction, neglect, or exaggeration. His call is to preach the Word in a way that is plainly and powerfully relevant to every aspect of life.

The Lord gives Jonah a new opportunity to prove the sincerity of his penitence by confronting him with the very task he earlier had evaded. This time, the prophet carries out the Lord's orders. He goes to the impressive city of Nineveh and delivers the message God has entrusted to him. He declares that the wrath of the Lord is about to be revealed from heaven against all the ungodliness and unrighteousness of the Ninevites (3:3-4). Jonah is not afraid of that formidable metropolis, so imposing in its power, dazzling in its wealth, notorious in its sin. He goes and preaches the word of the Lord to Nineveh.

Soon after a memorable evangelistic crusade in New York, Billy Graham said that the effective penetration of that great city was an extremely difficult task. He compared his efforts to those of a mosquito biting an elephant.

Why is it that we find church planting in the suburbs so challenging and the maintenance of an effective witness in urban centers so difficult and depressing? It's not easy to serve in a vast concentration of people from many backgrounds. How do you reach the busy, lonely, disillusioned, materialistic, and destitute who live there? How can we touch the lives of the sophisticated rich and the disappointed poor? The answers are not immediately apparent. Yet Jonah's experience clearly suggests that with our society's apparently irreversible trend toward urbanization, we need to budget adequate resources—human and material—for the evangelization of our cities.

Response. From the account given in Jonah (3:5-9), we know that the Ninevites were neither amused by the rantings of this frenzied foreigner, nor angered over the severe denunciations his message contained. Rather, they actually accepted his prophecy! They did not deny their guilt or try to blame extenuating circumstances, a polluted social environment, or heredity for their transgressions. The Ninevites responded with repentance. They listened to Jonah's preaching and "believed God" (3:5). They acknowledged that they deserved God's judgment and took steps to avert impending disaster:

• Instead of feasting, they fasted (3:5).
• All of them, from the greatest to the least, put on sackcloth as a sign of humiliation before God (3:5).
• Even the king laid aside his royal robes, covered himself with penitential garb, and sat in ashes (3:6).
• The king also issued a decree, together with his nobles, that man and beast were to show signs of humiliation before God and call urgently on Him for mercy (3:7-8).
• The king asked his subjects to give up their evil ways and their violence in response to Jonah's message about coming judgment (3:8).

God does not impose penance; He looks for repentance. A change of clothing from extravagant dress to sackcloth means absolutely nothing without an inward change of mind. It is not enough to fast *for* sin. We must fast *from* sin. Our ears must fast from slander, our eyes from pornography, our tongues from falsehood, our hands from violence, and our hearts from hatred.

What inspired the repentance of the Ninevites? Undoubtedly, the dread of coming doom caused them to think seriously about settling their accounts with God. But more than a fear of judgment was involved here. Their repentance also was prompted by the hope of God's mercy (3:9).

If the people of Nineveh repented at the preaching of Jonah, isn't it strange that so many persons refused to repent at the preaching of Jesus—the One greater than Jonah?

The men of Nineveh will stand up at the judgment with this generation and condemn it; for they repented at the preaching of Jonah, and now One greater than Jonah is here (Matt. 12:41).

A veteran missionary explained this "mystery of resistance" in the following terms:

If our Gospel is veiled, it is veiled to those who are perishing. The god of this age has blinded the minds of unbelievers, so that they cannot see the light of the Gospel of the glory of Christ, who is the image of God (2 Cor. 4:3-4).

Has God made His light shine in our hearts to give us a knowledge of His glory in the face of Christ? Then this privilege requires us to communicate the Gospel's truths to others (2 Cor. 4:6).

Forgiveness. The God who judges sin also forgives sinners. When He saw what the people of Nineveh did, and how they turned from their evil ways, He had compassion on them and did not bring the threatened destruction on them (Jonah 3:10). This is good news for sinful man. If we earnestly repent in response to His Word, He will forgive us (Isa. 55:6-7; Jer. 18:8; 1 John 1:9).

COMPASSION

God's compassion spared the Ninevites from threatened and deserved judgment. But this turn of events did not please Jonah at all! As a matter of fact, he was greatly displeased at God's decision.

Complaint. Jonah proceeds to tell God, "I told You so!" He claims that fear had nothing to do with his refusal to go to Nineveh. No, he wasn't terrified by the fierceness of the Assyrians. Actually, he had been turned off by the tenderness of the Lord! The petulant prophet protests:

O Lord, is not this what I said when I was still at home? That is why I was so quick to flee to Tarshish. I knew that You are a gracious and compassionate God, slow to anger and abounding in love, a God who relents from sending calamity. Now, O Lord, take away my life, for it is better for me to die than to live (Jonah 4:1-3).

Put yourself in Jonah's sandals. Try to understand him. He has been assigned to communicate God's words to the cruel, violent, rapacious Assyrians in Nineveh. But he wondered, "Why should they be warned to flee from the wrath to come? Why not let them be consumed in the fiery judgment they deserve?" Such thoughts betray a narrow, sectarian, exclusivist attitude—not unlike that of the elder brother in our Lord's parable who resented his loving father's gracious welcome of a returning prodigal.

Correction. Sarcasm, as well as humor, is evident in God's question to the sulking prophet: "Have you any right to be angry?" (4:4) If men have sinned against God and repented toward God, isn't it God's prerogative to pardon them? Why, then, should Jonah quarrel with the Lord and begrudge His crumbs of divine mercy to the Gentile world?

Jonah's narrow nationalism and resentment are in sharp contrast to the attitude of heaven's angels. They rejoice when even one sinner comes home to God (Luke 15:1-10). Jonah's anger also stands in absolute antithesis to Christ's tears over those who reject His saving grace (Luke 19:41-44). How different is Jonah's disposition from that of Him who is not willing that any should perish, but desires that all should come to repentance! (2 Peter 3:9)

Renewed Complaint Narrow-minded nationalists and sectarian extremists have a lesson to learn about the sovereign grace of our compassionate God. The Lord will teach Jonah this lesson in a most unusual way. He lets Jonah find shelter under the shadow of a vine that gives him comfort on a sultry day. Then the same Providence which provided the vine sends a worm to ruin it; Jonah once again is exposed to the withering blast of the sun. The Prophet reacts angrily to this incident, and claims that he is "angry enough to die" over the sudden loss of the vine! (Jonah 4:5-9)

Let us learn from this incident that our hearts should be set on the Lord who is the giver of all good things, rather than on the gifts He gives. Our highest happiness depends on God, not on the things that are received or lost in the course of His providence. Contentment comes to the person who honestly can say, "The Lord gave and the Lord has taken away; may the name of the Lord be praised" (Job 1:21).

Renewed Correction. In response to Jonah's second complaint, God once more corrects the insensitive critic of His love:

You have been concerned about this vine, though you did

not tend it or make it grow. . . . But Nineveh has more than a hundred and twenty thousand people who cannot tell their right hand from their left, and many cattle as well. Should I not be concerned about that great city? (Jonah 4:10)

If Jonah is this troubled over the loss of a mere vine that sprang up overnight and died just as quickly, should not God be moved with compassion over the predicament of a great city in danger of destruction? The answer is obvious.

In conclusion, Jonah could well serve as the patron saint of every self-righteous, narrow-minded nationalist who ever walked the earth. Such people have more concern for things than persons. They cannot get excited about sharing the Gospel with those who are "not of our kind." They wait for God to come around to their way of thinking, while He waits for them to come around to His way of loving.

The scribes and Pharisees portrayed in the Gospels were Jonah's heirs. They could not understand why Jesus mingled with publicans and sinners, cleansed the victims of leprosy, and welcomed into the fellowship of His company penitent prostitutes and transformed thieves.

Surely, we need to look at the world through the eyes of our compassionate Lord. When we begin to do this, we will see that there's a wideness in God's mercy like the wideness of the sea. Such a vision will renew our sense of mission and send us to our own Ninevehs with fresh zeal and tenderness.

SIX

"Forceful, descriptive style . . . consistent revelation of divine judgment, compassion, and hope . . . familiar with the corruptions of city life in Israel and Judah" (J.D. Douglas, ed., THE NEW BIBLE DICTIONARY, IVP, p. 819).

"God requires the fulfillment of duties: doing righteousness and exercising love. These two embrace all the commandments of the second table, of whose fulfillment Israel thought so little, that it was addicted to the very opposite— namely, injustice, oppression, and want of affection. . . . Without these moral virtues, sacrificial worship was a spiritless *opus operatum*, in which God had no pleasure" (C.F. Keil, THE TWELVE MINOR PROPHETS, Eerdmans, vol. 1, p. 497).

"Micah is brief in upbraiding, indignant in casting back the pleas of the false prophets, concise in his threatenings of woe, save where he lingers mournfully over the desolation, large and flowing in his descriptions of mercy to come. . . . Micah describes the future evangelic repentance, submission to, and waiting upon God and His righteousness, and God's free plenary forgiveness" (E.B. Pusey, THE MINOR PROPHETS, Funk & Wagnalls, p. 291).

"As One who delights in mercy, He will have compassion on Israel again, will tread down its sins . . . and cast them into the depths of the sea" (C.F. Keil, MINOR PROPHETS, vol. 1, p. 515).

MICAH
STRICTLY
THEOCENTRIC

ARE YOU INDIGNANT OVER INJUSTICE? I recently read of a man who was accused and convicted of kicking another man to death on the sidewalk outside a tavern. The victim was attacked and killed without any provocation whatsoever. Given only a three-year jail term, the criminal was put on day parole after serving a mere seven months of his sentence! Surely this turn of events casts the administration of criminal justice in a poor light, undermines the credibility of the appeal courts, and demands a complete review.

How do you react to falsehood? When seminary professors or those ordained to the ministry of the Word deny biblical inspiration and authority, do you simply accept their drift to doctrinal apostasy as inevitable? The church ought to be the pillar and ground of the truth. Yet when it accepts false teaching, it no longer supports the Gospel; the body of Christ becomes an accomplice to its subversion.

What about the new morality? Some psychologists claim that every one of the Ten Commandments may, and must, be broken in the name of "love." Even adultery can be committed to the glory of God. Practicing homosexuals and lesbians now come out of the closet and into the chancel. Their right to ordination is argued by masters of rationalization. What God's Word repeatedly and unmistakably calls sin is dismissed in favor of conformity to the declining standards of contemporary society.

There once was a man who encountered similar forms of corruption among the princes, priests, and prophets of his day. His name was Micah, and he cared enough about honesty to confront injustice, heresy, and immorality with high courage.

Micah of Moresheth received his message from the Lord during the reigns of Jotham, Ahaz, and Hezekiah, kings of Judah. He saw visions concerning Samaria (the Northern Kingdom, also known as Israel) and Jerusalem (capital of the Southern Kingdom of Judah) in the middle of the eighth century B.C. Micah's message shows an awareness of the political, economic, military, and religious signs of his times. But the prophet never loses sight of the absolute centrality of the true and living God in every event. Whatever pleases the Lord, whatever brings glory to Him and benefits His people, is good. Whatever and whoever disobeys Him, however, shall find ruin.

In short, Micah is a man who lives up to his name, which means "Who is like Jehovah?" He views everyone and everything in relation to God. Micah is strictly theocentric.

In particular, he declares:

(1) God's Greatness
(1:2-4; 3:8)

(2) God's Righteousness
A. Israel and Judah (1:5-16)
B. The Conspirators (2:1-5)
C. False Prophets (2:6-11; 3:5-7)
D. Evil Leaders (3:1-3, 9-10; 3:4, 11-12)
E. Inexcusable Ingratitude (6:1-5, 9-16)

(3) God's Goodness
A. Special Revelation (1:2; 3:8)
B. Promised Liberation (2:12-13; 4:6-10)
C. Messianic Expectation (5:2-5)
D. World Evangelization (4:1-5)

(4) God's Forgiveness
    A. The Revelation of Grace (7:18-20)
    B. The Response of Gratitude (6:6-8)

GOD'S GREATNESS

In a time when superpowers like Egypt and Assyria made Judah and Israel tremble, Micah kept the focus of his faith on God. He was overwhelmed with a sense of God's greatness, with the sovereign Lord who not only presides over His holy temple, but who governs the entire universe (1:2-4). While the heathen boasted about their gods and worshiped idols, Micah declared the uniqueness of the Lord, the Creator and sustainer of the world.

God's authority and power, Micah says, are as absolute as they are universal and eternal. He is the Lord of the whole earth, not merely a tribal deity limited to a few hills or narrow valleys. This great God works all things after the counsel of His will. His plan is destined to prevail. Long before the hymn was written, Micah the prophet exclaimed: "How great Thou art!" It is this great God who authorizes Micah to deliver His message. The prophet affirms:

> I am filled with power, with the Spirit of the Lord, and with justice and might, to declare to Jacob his transgression, to Israel his sin (3:8).

GOD'S RIGHTEOUSNESS

It sometimes happens that men of great power and authority abuse their positions for the furtherance of unworthy purposes. Numerous congressmen and parliamentarians have found themselves enmeshed in conflict-of-interest cases. Not even presidents are immune to the temptation to use smear tactics, break-ins, cover-ups, and dirty tricks to gain an unfair advantage over their rivals. The God Micah reveals, however, is known for His righteousness. The prophet declares that the Lord loves justice and calls people to account for their actions and attitudes. The sovereign Lord considers evidence impartially and completely. Accordingly, He is qualified to hold us responsible for what we think, say, or do. And so He judges the following groups:

Israel and Judah. God judges and condemns both Judah and Israel for their sins. Their radical evil is idolatry (1:5). God will punish this transgression and the transgressors shall be reduced to rubble with their idols (1:6-7). Such punishment brings sorrow to the prophet's soul. He weeps for the shame and pain of his people (1:8-16).

The Conspirators. God knows all about those who conspire secretly, who plan iniquity, who covet and defraud (2:1-2). The Lord will bring disaster on them, humble their pride, and take away their possessions (2:3-5).

False Prophets. The Lord who speaks is aware of those persons who would silence His servants and substitute false prophecy for truth and justice (2:6-11). They lead the people astray and confirm, rather than challenge, their prejudices (3:5). Therefore, the Lord will envelop them in thick darkness, disgrace them openly, and expose them as frauds (3:6-7).

Evil Leaders. Those who were to lead the kingdom are guilty of betraying their sacred trust. They should know justice and eagerly seek to practice it. But instead, they hate good and love evil. They despise what is right and use violence to gain their corrupt objectives (3:1-3, 9-10). The Lord will not listen to their prayers, because they have not penitently broken with the practice of evil (3:4). Their bribery and lying will bring judgment on themselves and the people they have misled (3:11-12).

Inexcusable Ingratitude. Like a prosecuting attorney, the Lord brings a ringing indictment against Israel. The charges He makes are serious. His case is strong. The people have experienced the Lord's deliverance from the slavery of Egypt and known His abundant provision during the wilderness journey to the Promised Land (6:1-5). Therefore, Israel's disobedience reflects the the peoples' profound ingratitude to God. Through Micah, the Lord again warns of coming judgment and total loss. Sin will bring restlessness and ruin (6:9-16).

GOD'S GOODNESS

Special Revelation. If Micah's portrait of God shows us His greatness and righteousness, it also reveals His goodness. The very fact that God speaks through Micah is a sure sign of His

benevolence (1:2; 3:8). Without that special, supernatural, redemptive revelation given through the prophets and climaxed
in Christ, we would be left to grope for answers to matters of
supreme importance (Heb. 1:1-2). Who is God? What are His
intentions toward us? What does He require of us? How can
we cope with our depravity and overcome our mortality?

God, in His goodness, gives us the answers to these questions in His Word. The entrance of His truth brings light to
our hearts and minds. We thus are spared from the futility of
guesswork, mere feeling, superstition, or speculation. We can,
instead, have certainty. Surely, this is a sign of God's
goodness.

Promised Liberation. The Lord who threatens judgment
and warns of disaster also promises deliverance. He will gather the remnant of Israel as a shepherd gathers his flock. He
will guard, as well as guide and govern, His gathered people
(Micah 2:12-13). If they are to be carried away into captivity
when God manifests His wrath, they will be brought back
from exile when He demonstrates His grace (4:6-10).

On a deeper level, however, the liberation being discussed
here does not merely involve Assyria and Babylon, but deals
with sin and death. The father of John the Baptist referred to
this fact when he said that the Lord gives His people salvation
from their enemies in order that they might serve Him "without fear in holiness and righteousness" (Luke 1:74-75). The
ultimate rescue, redemption, and release for which men look
is from the condemnation and corruption of sin, the power of
the evil one, and the finality of death. We are offered these
through faith in the liberating Lord Jesus Christ, "because of
the tender mercy of our God" (Luke 1:78).

Messianic Expectation. This redemption will come about
through the Messiah. Micah prophesies:

> But you, Bethlehem Ephrathah, though you are small
> among the clans of Judah, out of you will come for Me One
> who will be ruler over Israel, whose origins are from of old,
> from ancient times (Micah 5:2).

The promised Saviour, born in Bethlehem ("the house of
bread"), comes to feed the deepest hunger of the human heart.

He also comes to rule His people. Their security is in His sovereignty. He is born into the world at Bethlehem, but exists from everlasting to everlasting (John 1:1, 14).

Concerning this coming liberator, Micah says:

> He will stand and shepherd His flock in the strength of the Lord, in the majesty of the name of the Lord His God. And they will live securely, for then His greatness will reach to the ends of the earth. And He will be their peace (Micah 5:4-5).

Like David, the Messiah will be a shepherd-king. He will use His authority and power for the good of those entrusted to His care. We know that this prophecy was fulfilled in Jesus' birth at Bethlehem (Matt. 2:5-6). Now, He "delivers His people from the captivity of sin and death, and unites them in one fellowship. He is the Prince of Peace" (S.F. Winward, *A Guide to the Prophets*, Hodder & Stoughton, p. 71).

The quest for peace in our own time is difficult and distressing. At the international level, we encounter the problem of maintaining a defense posture which is strong enough to deter potential aggression, but which does not actually provoke attack. The threat of nuclear war, like a malignant cloud, overshadows human existence on this planet. Yet Christ can make a difference even in this area.

During the closing years of the nineteenth century, Chile and Argentina agreed to settle their long-standing boundary disputes through arbitration. To mark that amicable settlement, they placed a massive statue of Christ on a high mountain in the Andes. The statue's base bears this inscription:

> Sooner shall these mountains crumble into dust than Chileans and Argentinians shall break this peace which at the feet of Christ, the Redeemer, they have sworn to keep.

Peace at every level, whether between nations, races, or within churches and families, depends on submission to Him who is our peace (Micah 5:5).

World evangelization. According to Isaiah, during the messianic age, the nations of the world will come in pilgrimage to

Jerusalem, to be taught by the Lord so that they might live their lives in accordance with His Word (Isa. 2:2-4). What we read in Isaiah also is found in Micah (4:1-5). Both prophets emphasize that the nations will be attracted to Jerusalem because it is the center from which God's redemptive revelation radiates. Listening to the law of the Lord, believing the Gospel of grace, submitting to the King's authority, men will discover the secret of peace. Now they can beat their swords into plowshares and their spears into pruning hooks.

In the New Testament, however, the movement of the nations with reference to Jerusalem is reversed. The renewed community of God's people will go from Jerusalem into Judea, Samaria, and the ends of the earth with the Word. What Isaiah and Micah spoke of as being centripetal, Christ and His apostles recast as centrifugal (Matt. 28:18-20; Luke 24:47; John 20:21; Acts 1:8). But Micah's prophecy still will be fulfilled through the involvement of those whom God has forgiven and redeemed. By their words and service—as they walk in the Lord's ways—they will attract the nations to Him.

GOD'S FORGIVENESS

The Revelation of Grace. Micah marvels at the manifestation of God's amazing grace. He exclaims:

> Who is a God like You, who pardons sin and forgives the transgression of the remnant of His inheritance? You do not stay angry forever but delight to show mercy. You will again have compassion on us; You will tread our sins underfoot and hurl all our iniquities into the depths of the sea. You will be true to Jacob, and show mercy to Abraham, as You pledged an oath to our fathers in days long ago (Micah 7:18-20).

It is sometimes alleged that the God of the Old Testament— in contrast to the God revealed in the New—is all severity, wrath, and judgment. Nothing could be further from the truth! Just as the Lord of the New Testament abounds in steadfast love as well as justice, so the God Micah portrays pardons sin, forgives transgression, and delights to show mercy.

Samuel Davies (1723-1761), president of Princeton University in colonial America, wrote a fine Gospel hymn, "Great God of Wonders," based on this portion of Micah's prophecy:

> Great God of wonders! all Thy ways
> Are worthy of Thyself—divine;
> But the bright glories of Thy grace
> Beyond Thine other wonders shine:
>
> Who is a pardoning God like Thee?
> Or who has grace so rich and free?
>
> Pardon—from an offended God!
> Pardon—for sins of deepest dye!
> Pardon—bestowed through Jesus' blood!
> Pardon—that brings the rebel nigh!
>
> Who is a pardoning God like Thee?
> Or who has grace so rich and free?

This is evangelical hymnology at its best; it presents the biblical message of God's forgiving grace flowing to guilty sinners who dare to believe His promise. Here is a truly theocentric hymn. Its focus is on the God of sovereign grace, rather than on the fluctuating feelings and psychological states of self-centered creatures.

We come to a true knowledge of ourselves only as we know God and discern our relationship to Him. Let us learn to live theocentrically, evaluating our standards, motivations, and goals in the light of God.

The Response of Gratitude. God's amazing grace calls for us to respond with a grateful heart. The Lord who pardons sin and forgives transgression looks for more than mere external religion and the performance of ritual on the part of His people. The prophet asks:

> With what shall I come before the Lord and bow down before the exalted God? Shall I come before Him with burnt offerings, with calves a year old? Will the Lord be pleased with thousands of rams, with ten thousand rivers of oil? Shall I offer my firstborn for my transgression, the

fruit of my body for the sin of my soul? (Micah 6:6-7)

Then comes the answer:

He has showed you, O man, what is good. And what does the Lord require of you? To act justly and to love mercy and to walk humbly with your God (6:8).

Centuries before, other prophets had declared that obedience was better than the mere ritual performance of sacrifice. Amos called for justice in the social order; Hosea emphasized mercy; Isaiah stressed holiness. Now Micah blends these notes into a richer, fuller melody:

● Act justly: instead of clamoring for your rights, recognize what you owe others and give them their due.
● Love mercy: do not respond to human weakness and brokenness with contempt, but with a compassion that really cares.
● Walk humbly: renounce all arrogance, remembering your relationship of dependence and submission to the holy God.

The prophet presents biblical ethics in a context of grace. That is, he shows us that we cannot merit salvation by acting justly or loving mercy. Our imperfect works can never earn salvation. But God has saved us by His grace. To express our gratitude to Him, we must be obedient to His loving-kindness (Eph. 2:8-10).

SEVEN

"Nahum is both very sour and very sure about Assyria's doom, and one feels that as God had given him reason to be sure, so the Ninevites had given him reason to be sour; something seems to have roused the prophet considerably" (Hubert Van Zeller, THE OUTSPOKEN ONES, Sheed and Ward, pp. 93-94).

"The book of Nahum contains one extended prophecy concerning Nineveh, in which the ruin of that city and the Assyrian world-power is predicted. [Yet Jehovah,] the zealous God and avenger of evil . . . proves Himself as a refuge to those who trust in Him" (C.F. Keil, THE TWELVE MINOR PROPHETS, Eerdmans, vol. 2, p. 4).

"The prophecy of Nahum is both the complement and the counterpart of the book of Jonah. [While Jonah recalls the mercy of God to penitent Nineveh, Nahum confronts impenitent Ninevites with] the aweful side of the attributes of God" (E.B. Pusey, THE MINOR PROPHETS, Funk & Wagnalls, p. 356).

"It was his object to show that God had a care for that kingdom, on account of his adoption or covenant; though the Israelites had perfidiously separated themselves from the people of God, yet God's covenant remained in force. His design then was to show that God was the Father and protector of that kingdom" (John Calvin, COMMENTARIES ON THE MINOR PROPHETS, Calvin Translation Society, vol. 3, p. 414).

NAHUM THEOLOGICAL EQUILIBRIUM

THE EXOTIC LAND of Kuala Lumpur teems with Malays, Chinese, Indians, Arabs, Eurasians, and Europeans. Its mosques and temples are evidence of the Islamic, Buddhist, and Hindu faiths dominant there. During the festival of Thaipusam, usually at the end of January, devotees of Hinduism fulfill their personal vows by walking in a seven-mile procession to the Batu Caves, wearing *kavadi*. These are yoke-like frames of wood or steel, spiked and hooked into the flesh. Some of the pilgrims have long spears skewered through their tongues and cheeks. Others walk through fire as an act of religious devotion. They believe that God requires such behavior from His creatures.

Some persons, conversely, are convinced that the Deity exists solely to gratify the wishes and whims of His children; He indulges them with a benevolence bordering on permissiveness; He makes no demands and imposes no discipline.

These conflicting—and erroneous—interpretations show us that our view of God—and His view of us—are of the utmost, importance to our spiritual well being.

Nahum the Elkoshite portrays the true and living God in a most balanced way. Though his prophecy was first delivered against the powerful Assyrian capital of Nineveh—notorious for its arrogance and aggression—it presents us with a wonderful vision of the Lord as the God of both justice and grace.

In response to Jonah's preaching during the eighth century B.C., Nineveh had shown signs of repentance. God's threatened judgment thus was averted (Jonah 3:1-10). Yet now, in the time of Nahum, Nineveh seems to have resumed its evil ways. The sentence suspended by a merciful God is about to be carried out as the Lord expresses His justice. When men and nations reject God's grace, they inevitably must face His wrath.

Nahum addresses this, and other subjects, as follows:

(1) **God Judges**
   A. Righteous Indignation (1:1-6, 8-14)
   B. Threatened Humiliation (2:1-13)
   C. Justified Destruction (3:1-19)

(2) **God Saves**
   A. Punishment and Patience (1:3)
   B. Condemnation and Compassion (1:7)
   C. Affliction and Assurance (1:12-13, 15)

GOD JUDGES

In language that is both vivid and forceful, Nahum describes the holy God who will not coexist everlastingly with moral evil. Sin is so repugnant in His sight that it must be followed with judgment.

Righteous Indignation. Nahum's lyric poetry paints a picture of the character of God worthy of prolonged contemplation. The Lord, he says, is a jealous God who takes vengeance against His enemies (1:2). He is the God of holiness, not permissiveness. The Lord takes sin seriously. It is an assault on His majesty, a challenge to His authority, a defilement of His creation, to treat violations of His laws lightly.

God's omnipotence supports His justice; the wicked are not declared innocent—they are condemned. Yet God's wrath is not the arbitrary whim or capricious manifestation of someone who is irrational and vindictive. Our God is slow to anger (1:3) and He moves in judgment only after repeated warnings. When men despise the Lord's patience and take advantage of His forbearance to continue sinning, they will find that He is great in power and unerring in judgment.

The God who reveals Himself through Nahum's prophecy is the Judge of the universe. As one commentator has observed:

> He cannot be persuaded either by flattery or force to declare any transgressor of His law free of guilt. Nor will He remit the penalty of anyone deserving punishment. . . . He also has unlimited power to execute such judgment (Theodore Laetsch, *The Minor Prophets*, Concordia, p. 297).

The prophet also notes that whirlwind, storm, and cloud serve His righteous purpose. He rebukes seas and rivers; mountains quake at His approach, and hills melt in the presence of the God who is a consuming fire (Nahum 1:3-6).

Who can stand before such indignation, kindled against sin? Who can abide the fury and fierceness of His anger over man's failure to love? God surely will put an end to oppression, and devour tyrants like stubble. Do the wicked conspire against Him? They shall be frustrated and cut down (1:8-14).

Threatened Humiliation. Mighty Nineveh must reckon with the Almighty God. He once spared the Assyrian capital when it repented after hearing Jonah's preaching. Judgment was averted—then. But now, with the resumption of sin, the suspended sentence becomes operative again. Chariots and horsemen, defensive walls and wealthy palaces, generals and engineers—none of these can turn aside the judgment of God. Plundered treasure, paralyzing fear, broken power—these shall be the lot of all who in their fatal foolishness dare to align themselves against the Almighty (2:1-13).

Take a closer look at this threatened destruction. The proud capital of the Assyrian Empire is warned of coming judgment. Nineveh shall be invaded and its people scattered in humiliating defeat. The Lord who is sovereign will use other nations as instruments to inflict punishment on a city and empire whose ferocity and rapacity had brought ruin to so many. Assyria will lose its dominance among the nations and will be replaced by the Babylonians, Medes, and Persians. But because of these developments, the deported Israelites will be able to return from exile to their ancestral land (2:1-2). Once again, God's sovereign plan is at work!

Nahum now continues his prophecy of coming woes. Nineveh, he proclaims, is doomed to destruction. An empire that seems formidable and unconquerable shall eventually collapse and crumble (2:3-6). The proud triumphalism of the past will become painful humiliation as possessions are plundered and people enslaved (2:7-12). Totalitarian nations whose power and wealth are the rewards of aggression inevitably must reckon with the Ultimate Opponent: the Lord Almighty (2:13).

Justified Destruction. The God who speaks through Nahum does not tolerate the violence of a city where life is cheap, robbery is common, and lies are the stuff of business and politics (3:1-19).

Today, we are shocked when we hear that such crimes are committed in our society. We react with dismay when we learn of:

● Children who are physically and sexually abused by parents, relatives, and foster parents.
● Lawyers who defraud aged and handicapped clients.
● Industrialists who are held for ransom.
● Policemen who are murdered in the line of duty.
● Terrorists who bomb a bank, department store, or embassy to extort by force that which they could never attain by ballot.

But are we startled when moral evil is *institutionalized* and finds expression on a vast scale? People can speak of the Holocaust—the state-sponsored elimination of 6 million Jews—without the slightest shudder! That grim manifestation of racism and genocide, implemented as government policy, is for many a mere statistic.

Similarly, think of how lawmakers increasingly are accepting and encouraging the practice of abortion. In the past decade, at least 15 million lives were snuffed out in North America alone as a result of abortion. As legislators and pressure groups argue for abortion on demand, our society seems insensitive to the fact that the destruction of the embryo is a violation of the divine right to life. If this trend continues, we inevitably will see the legalization of infanticide and euthanasia as well.

The true and living God will not ignore such moral evil. As Nahum points out, He draws near to judge; the slumbering rulers of Assyria will be overtaken. Its ignoble nobles shall be cast into the dust of defeat and disgrace. Like the fortified Egyptian city of Thebes that fell to Ashurbanipal in 661 B.C. (3:8-10), Nineveh also will collapse—regardless of its formidable defenses (3:14-19).

History shows that this prophecy was fulfilled in 612 B.C. when the Babylonians under Nebuchadnezzer devastated Nineveh. Today, in the land of Iraq, on the eastern bank of the river Tigris, and opposite the city of Mosul, all that remains of proud Nineveh are two large mounds surrounded by crumbling walls. The righteousness of God ensures the inevitable ruin of nations and civilizations that dare to violate His moral order.

We need to remember this fact. We must see God as portrayed in Nahum's vision, perfect in His holiness, awesome in might, majesty, and execution of justice. A failure to take these divine attributes seriously makes for a shallow sense of sin and thus for a cheap view of grace. It encourages a mere "believism" divorced from heartbroken repentance and a genuine awareness of the hell-deservedness of sin. Nahum forcefully states that God finds sin repugnant and will bring retribution where repentance is absent.

GOD SAVES

Punishment and Patience. If Nahum reveals the God who judges, he also makes known the Lord who saves. The prophet proclaims both the message of punishment *and* the word of patience. He notes that though the people provoke God by persisting in disobedience, the Lord is "slow to anger" (1:3). With amazing forbearance, God gives us time to see our mistakes and return to Him. He is the waiting Father, looking for the prodigal to come home again.

Think of our Lord's patience with doubting Thomas, impulsive Peter, and hot-tempered James and John. Consider His patience as He holds back judgment so that none should perish, but all might come to repentance (2 Peter 3:9). God forbid that we should show contempt for the riches of His tolerance and patience by not realizing that His kindness is meant to lead us toward repentance (Rom. 2:4).

Condemnation and Compassion. The God Nahum describes in such vivid colors is opposed to evil; but He also is open to receive all who turn to Him for help:

> The Lord is good, a refuge in times of trouble. He cares for those who trust in Him, but with an overwhelming flood He will make an end of Nineveh; He will pursue His foes into darkness (Nahum 1:7).

This is theological equilibrium, in that Nahum presents a balanced doctrine of God. As Theodore Laetsch writes, "Rarely is the absolute, essential unity of divine attributes, which to the human mind seem contradictory opposites, brought out as forcefully as in this passage." Here we see the fury of God's holy displeasure against sin and the wonder of His lovingkindness. We are face to face with Him "whose wrath is as boundless as His grace, whose mercy is as limitless as His anger" (*The Minor Prophets*, Concordia, p. 296).

Affliction and Assurance. When the Lord chastises His people He does it in love. And when that discipline has accomplished His good purpose, He will afflict them no more (Nahum 1:12). By the demonstration of His gracious might, He will break the yoke of bondage and set His people free (1:13).

God did this very thing at the time of the Exodus, when He liberated Israel from the slavery of Egypt. He will do it again as the grip of Babylon is broken and the exiles are allowed to return to the Promised Land. This is good news for the oppressed. Let those whom the Lord sets free rejoice in their redemption and celebrate God's goodness by keeping their solemn feasts and fulfilling their sacred vows (1:15).

Our study of Nahum's prophecy reminds us that the truth of God's grace must not be isolated from the reality of His justice. Nahum affirms both—with an admirable sense of balance.

Today, the church needs to recover a sense of theological equilibrium by hearing all that the prophets have spoken and understanding all that the apostles teach. We must avoid the tendency to follow a smorgasbord approach to Scripture, picking out only what seems to confirm our prejudices and conveniently leaving everything else aside.

Consider the beautiful balance of biblical revelation. Scripture speaks of:

- The unity *and* triunity of God.
- The transcendence *and* immanence of God.
- The sovereignty of God *and* the responsibility of man.
- The deity *and* humanity of Jesus Christ.
- The necessity of evangelism *and* social concern.
- The work of Christ for us *and* that of the Spirit in us.
- The wages of sin (death) *and* the gift of God (eternal life).

The consequence of stressing only one aspect of biblical revelation and neglecting its complementary or supplementary truth is distortion. Think of the consequences of teaching only the holiness and justice of God. You could end up with a caricature of the Creator. He would be relentless, harsh, judgmental, and vindictive—One who delights in the destruction of the depraved.

Or suppose that you focus exclusively on the love, patience, and grace of God. Then you run the risk of turning His fatherly kindness into mere permissiveness. You've manufactured a God who gratifies the self-centered in their self-indulgence, forbids no evil by any authoritative command, accepts the relativistic ethics of the new morality, and fails to express His holiness in the punishment of sin.

Fortunately, Nahum points the way to a balanced view of God. Our theology, drawing on the fullness of God's self-revelation in the written Word and the Word made flesh, also should reflect the wholeness of His truth.

EIGHT

"He was a philosophical prophet, who, looking out on the history-making events of his day, asked why the ruthless overcame the righteous and whether goodness paid" (M.S. and J.L. Miller, eds., HARPER'S BIBLE DICTIONARY, Harper & Brothers, p. 239).

"The burden of the prophet is that of the problems of permitted evil, and the using of the Chaldeans as the instrument to scourge evildoers less wicked than themselves. [His prophecy opens] in mystery and questioning, it closes in certainty and affirmation" (G. Campbell Morgan, THE ANALYZED BIBLE, F.H. Revell, p. 323).

"The book falls into three major parts, corresponding to the three chapters. Chapter one announces the terrible judgment of God that will come through the Chaldeans. Chapter two contains a five-fold lament, in which the Prophet announces the destruction of this proud, high-handed, idolatrous world power. Chapter three concludes with a hymn of praise to the mighty God, who is appearing in His majesty and power as the supreme Judge" (Ludwig Fuerbringer, THE ETERNAL WHY, Concordia, p. 5).

"Habakkuk comes to see that a man's arrogance carries within it the seed of his ruin, whereas the faithful man is assured of living in the light of God's favor" (J.D. Douglas, ed., THE NEW BIBLE DICTIONARY, IVP, p. 496).

"Habakkuk is eminently the prophet of reverential, awe-filled faith. This is the soul and center of his prophecy" (E.B. Pusey, THE MINOR PROPHETS, Funk & Wagnalls, p. 397).

HABAKKUK PHILOSOPHY OF HISTORY

SHAKESPEARE'S MACBETH DESCRIBES LIFE as a tale told by an idiot, full of sound and fury, signifying nothing. This causes us to wonder: Does life really lack meaning? Some people are genuinely convinced that history simply goes 'round and 'round in endless, futile cycles.

Others see history as do the disciples of Karl Marx: Class struggle and violent revolution, designed to overthrow the middle class and establish the dictatorship of the proletariat.

The Prophet Habakkuk scanned the signs of his times and was also perplexed by history. He wondered why, in a universe ruled by a righteous God, sinners were able to survive and succeed. Habakkuk struggled with the problem of history—but he eventually moved from a position of doubt to one of affirmation. He developed a philosophy of history through dialogue with God and expressed his convictions in prayer.

Habakkuk's prophetic message, however, probably is best known for several quotations. One often is used as a call to worship:

The Lord is in His holy temple; let all the earth be silent before Him (Hab. 2:20).

Another encourages worldwide missions, promising that:

The earth will be filled with the knowledge of the glory of the Lord, as the waters cover the sea (2:14).

Best known, of course, is the phrase that became the grand slogan of the Reformation:

The righteous will live by his faith (2:4).

But Habakkuk's message contains much more than these quotable quotes. As mentioned earlier, it gives us a biblical view of history:

(1) A Prophet's Perplexity (1:1-4)

(2) The Lord's Reply (1:5-11)

(3) A Prophet's Questions (1:12—2:1)

(4) The Lord's Answer
    A. The Righteous Will Live by Faith (2:2-4)
    B. As the Waters Cover the Sea (2:5-14)
    C. Let All the Earth Be Silent (2:15-20)

(5) A Prophet's Prayer
    A. Dependence (3:1-2)
    B. Reverence (3:3-15)
    C. Confidence (3:16-19)

A PROPHET'S PERPLEXITY

Habakkuk, whose name means "embrace," was God's messenger to Judah. He was sent with a warning about the coming invasion of the Babylonians (Chaldeans), whom God would employ as the agent of His judgment.

Habakkuk looks at the people in Judah who profess to believe in God. They have been given the Law of the Lord to direct them in life's relationships. Yet they ignore God's commandments and fail to practice justice. Indeed, the wicked surround the righteous, justice is perverted, iniquity abounds, and violence is the tragic consequence of contention and strife (1:1-4).

We face a similar situation today. How can we tell the pollsters that ours is a Christian nation—that we believe in God—that we consider ourselves to be a religious people—and yet have such a high incidence of violence? A number of our major cities report more homicides in one year than some European countries record in five. Think of the carnage on our highways, especially those injuries and deaths related to drunk drivers. Or consider the escalation of separation, abandonment, and divorce—all of which are taking a terrible toll on spouses, children, and grandparents. And yet we consider ourselves "A Christian Country" in contrast to other nations. How long will God put up with our sinfulness?

Where *is* God while all this is happening? Habakkuk is perplexed, and so are we. How can a God of sovereignty and purity permit such evil to exist in the lives of those who claim to be His people? Why doesn't He do something about this deteriorating situation?

These are questions that agitate not only the godly, but those who are critical of Christianity. If there *is* a good and all-powerful God, they argue, why doesn't He take some dramatic action to stop the growth of evil?

THE LORD'S REPLY

The Lord resolves Habakkuk's perplexity. However, His reply sounds strange, causes the prophet to wonder, and leaves him stunned.

First, the Lord states that He is not at all ignorant of, or indifferent to, the sins of those who profess to be His people. Those sins will be punished. How? Retribution, He says, will come through a pagan nation providentially raised up as the instrument of His chastisement. The Lord will allow the Babylonians—that fierce and impetuous people, dreaded and feared—to invade the Promised Land (1:5-7). Even though the Babylonians are "a law to themselves and promote their own honor" (1:7), they still are under the sovereign direction of the Lord of history for the accomplishment of His purposes.

According to God's description of them, their horses are swifter than leopards, and their cavalry fiercer than wolves at dusk. They swoop down like vultures in search of prey, and advance as irresistibly as a desert wind. They mock at kings, break through defenses, take prisoners, and credit idols with their triumphs (1:8-11).

A PROPHET'S QUESTIONS

This information from the Lord only intensifies the prophet's bewilderment. Habakkuk ponders the problem seriously. True, we deserve to be disciplined because we have turned away from God and committed many sins, he thinks. But why in the world will God use pagan nations to execute judgment on the descendants of Abraham? How can a holy God tolerate the treacherous and let the heathen defeat us? Won't this simply inflate the egos of the ungodly and lead them to praise their idols for another victory won? (1:12-17)

Surely, some of these questions have disturbed us as they did Habakkuk. We are a nation that claims to be Christian. Perhaps we deserve *some* discipline. But how can a God who is holy and righteous allow the Muslim and Communist countries of the world to ruin the economies and invade the borders of people traditionally considered a part of "the Christian West"? Doesn't His cause stand or fall with our survival?

The prophet ponders, wonders, and waits for God's answer to his complaint (2:1). And so must we.

THE LORD'S ANSWER

The Righteous Will Live by Faith. The Lord finally answers His servant. He says that those who glory in their strength and commit acts of aggression shall be held guilty in His sight. The Babylonians, who were used to chastise the covenant people, will themselves be punished for their violence and arrogance. But believers—those who trust humbly in the Lord—shall live. The people of faith will be considered righteous and survive His judgment (2:2-4).

It is in this context of the judgment of proud pagans and the preservation of righteous believers, that a most memorable phrase is first uttered: "The righteous will live by his faith" (2:4).

We can learn much about Habakkuk's prophecy by seeing how this famous statement was used in the New Testament and by Protestant Reformers.

This text is quoted several times in the New Testament. For

example, in a discussion of the duty of perseverance under pressure, one writer declares:

> You need to persevere so that when you have done the will of God, you will receive what He has promised. For in just a very little while, "He who is coming will come and will not delay. But My righteous one will live by faith. And if he shrinks back, I will not be pleased with him." But we are not of those who shrink back and are destroyed, but of those who believe and are saved (Heb. 10:36-39).

Faith perseveres, whatever the difficulties and temptations. Faith pleases God. Without such trust, it is impossible to please Him. The eleventh chapter of the Letter to the Hebrews goes on to recall the heroes of faith, and then refers to the trusting endurance of Jesus Christ. He is the Pioneer and Perfecter of our faith, "who for the joy set before Him endured the cross, scorning its shame, and sat down at the right hand of the throne of God" (Heb. 12:2).

Again, Paul incorporates Habakkuk's statement into his presentation of the Gospel and the truth of grace. He writes:

> All who rely on observing the Law are under a curse, for it is written: "Cursed is everyone who does not continue to do everything written in the Book of the Law." Clearly no one is justified before God by the Law, because, "The righteous will live by faith" (Gal. 3:10-11).

There are only two ways to be considered righteous in the sight of God. One is to obey all His commands perfectly and earn the status of righteousness. The other is to rely on the merits of Another, the perfect obedience of Jesus Christ. As sinners, we no longer can take this first route to righteousness. The only way left to those who want to get right with God is through faith, trust, and reliance on Jesus Christ.

The Apostle Paul also quotes Habakkuk in connection with his teaching on God's plan of salvation. Paul proudly declares:

> I am not ashamed of the Gospel, because it is the power of

God for the salvation of everyone who believes: first for the Jew, then for the Gentile. For in the Gospel a righteousness from God is revealed, a righteousness that is by faith from first to last, just as it is written: "The righteous will live by faith" (Rom. 1:16-17).

This passage, as mentioned earlier, also was basic to the Protestant Reformation. The message of justification by faith in Christ, the truth that sinners could attain acquittal and acceptance in God's sight through reliance on Christ, came as good news to many. People no longer needed to strive to wipe out their demerits by reciting prayers, observing rituals, or giving money to build shrines.

Martin Luther defined Habakkuk's concept of justification by faith with striking clarity:

By the one solid rock which we call the doctrine of justification, we mean that we are redeemed from sin, death, and the devil and are made partakers of life eternal, not by ourselves ... but by help from without, by the only-begotten Son of God, Jesus Christ. The article of justification, which is our only protection against all the powers and plottings of men, and the gates of hell, is this: by faith alone in Christ, without works, are we declared just and saved (E.M. Plass, ed., *What Luther Says*, Concordia, vol. 2, p. 701).

This great truth also is the theme of some familiar hymns. In "The Solid Rock," Edward Mote (1797-1874) put it this way:

> My hope is built on nothing less
> Than Jesus' blood and righteousness;
> I dare not trust the sweetest frame,
> But wholly lean on Jesus' name.
> On Christ, the solid Rock, I stand;
> All other ground is sinking sand.

Or think of the words of Nicolaus Ludwig Von Zinzendorf (1703-1791), as translated by John Wesley:

Jesus, Thy blood and righteousness
My beauty are, my glorious dress;
Midst flaming worlds, in these arrayed,
With joy shall I lift up my head.

Bold shall I stand in Thy great day;
For who aught to my charge shall lay?
Fully absolved through these I am
From sin and fear, from guilt and shame.

As the Waters Cover the Sea. While the righteous shall live
because of their faith in the living God, woes await the proud
Babylonians. Their ill-gotten gains will become the plunder
of rebellious captives. The very violence they used against
others will wreak havoc on them. God hates iniquity. With
His fiery judgment He will judge the polluted world. His
grand design, though, is that someday the earth shall be filled
with the knowledge of His glory, as the waters cover the sea
(Hab. 2:5-14).

The truth is, that in God's moral order, pride shall be broken and humbled in the dust. "Pride goes before destruction,
a haughty spirit before a fall" (Prov. 16:18). So it is with
Babylon:

Tyranny is self-destructive: the oppressor evokes the resistance which eventually brings about his downfall. In less
than a century the new Babylonian empire disappeared. He
whose soul was puffed up and not straight within him
came to his inevitable end (S.F. Winward, *A Guide to the
Prophets*, Hodder & Stoughton, pp. 119-120).

Meanwhile, God's kingdom shall increase. All the earth
will be filled with the knowledge of His glory, as the promised Saviour comes into the world and His Gospel is proclaimed to the ends of the earth (Matt. 28:18-20; Luke 24:47;
Acts 1:8).

Let All the Earth Be Silent. The Babylonians who disgraced
others shall themselves be humiliated. Devastation and terror
shall surely come upon them. Their idols will prove utterly
powerless to save them in the day of God's judgment. The

Lord plainly will reveal Himself as sovereign. His decision is final. No one can appeal His verdict to a higher authority. Let all the earth, Habakkuk declares, be silent before Him (2:15-20).

We need this reminder in a world where so many forces can impress, oppress, and depress us. We must recover the vision of God's majesty and see all else in the light of His sovereignty. Even when we cannot understand the design He is fulfilling in our lives, we still need to keep silence in His presence. God works out everything in conformity to the purpose of His will (Eph. 1:11).

A Prophet's Prayer

Habakkuk now understands that the Lord of history will discipline His people through pagan armies, but that the triumph of the ungodly is only temporary. The proud, idolatrous, and violent aggressor will himself be punished in God's own time. The faithful who rely on the Lord shall not perish; the righteous will live by their trust in God.

Realizing all this, Habakkuk is now encouraged to pray. He pours out his heart to God for things in keeping with the Lord's will. The prophet's prayer expresses deep convictions about the character of God and His dealings with both the covenant people and the nations. It is a prayer whose keynotes are dependence, reverence, and confidence.

Dependence. The prophet stands in awe of the Almighty and asks Him to do what He deems best. Habakkuk pleads, though, for God to remember mercy in the midst of wrath. While the sins of the people deserve the Lord's judgment, the Lord *has* promised mercy; Habakkuk recognizes God's right to inflict punishment, but he also reminds the Lord of His gracious offer to forgive the sins of the penitent (Hab. 3:1-2).

In effect, Habakkuk is asking God to take action. We can do the same. Are we concerned because the public worship of God is neglected? Are we disturbed because God's moral law is ignored, amended, or even defied by those who profess to be His people? Are we upset when churches spend most of their budgets on themselves and show little interest in world evangelization and social concern? We are not alone. God knows and cares about these things, and we *can* ask Him to instill a sense of renewal and reform in the church. Let us make our appeal to Him with humble dependence and be willing for His work to begin in us, no matter what the cost.

Reverence. With vivid imagery, Habakkuk describes a theophany—a visible manifestation of the true and living God (3:3-15). He marvels at the majesty of God, the Holy One whose splendor covers the heavens and whose praise resounds throughout the earth. He beholds the sunlike radiance of the Lord, the rays that flash from His omnipotent hand. As a result of this vision, the prophet again sees that the Lord of history can use plague or pestilence in the course of His providence for the fulfillment of a moral purpose. Judgment, chastisement, salvation—these are the ends of God's dealings with men and nations.

Do we share Habakkuk's view of God? Or is our God too small to deal with crucial issues and problems?

J.B. Phillips, best known for his admirable paraphrase of the New Testament, comments:

> The trouble with many people today is that they have not found a God big enough for modern needs. While their experience of life has grown in a score of directions, and their mental horizons have been expanded to the point of bewilderment by world events and scientific discoveries, their ideas of God have remained largely static (*Your God Is Too Small*, Wyvern Books, p. 7).

Is our God too small to meet the perplexity, purposelessness, and powerlessness that oppress us? Is that God too small to do justice to the revelation of the Almighty given in Holy Scripture? We must learn to see Him as He is portrayed in the Word, and respond to Him with deepest reverence.

Confidence. Habakkuk's final words are vibrant with an optimism that is based on the sovereignty and goodness of God (Hab. 3:16-19). There may be much in life that can bring discouragement and dismay to those who seriously survey conditions in the church and on the political scene; but we can be spared from pessimism by thinking on the greatness and grace of God.

Think particularly of these confident words:

Though the fig tree does not bud and there are no grapes on the vines, though the olive crop fails and the fields produce no food, though there are no sheep in the pen and no cattle in the stalls, yet I will rejoice in the Lord, I will be joyful in God my Saviour (3:17-18).

The poet William Cowper (1731-1800) spent much of his life on the edge of despair. At times, the power of depression gripped him so strongly that he believed suicide might be his only way out. But friends like John Newton—the author of "Amazing Grace"—gave him wise counsel and pointed him to scriptural consolation. It was then that God's warm, clear light broke through the darkness that surrounded Cowper. Contemplating the confident words of Habakkuk, he wrote:

> Though vine nor fig-tree neither
>   Their wonted fruit should bear,
> Though all the field should wither,
>   Nor flocks nor herds be there;
> Yet, God the same abiding,
>   His praise shall tune my voice;
> For while in Him confiding,
>   I cannot but rejoice.

It may be easy to sing Cowper's words when everything is going well. But what do you do in the crises of life? We may face a job transfer that involves relocation and dislocation, or periods of unemployment. A physician may tell you that your malignancy needs surgery. A dear friend or member of the family dies. What then?

We would be less than human if we experienced no feeling of sadness or pain in life's adversities. Yet if we are sincerely dependent, reverent, and confident, we can experience sacred joy in God our Saviour. Confirming Habakkuk's prophecy, the Apostle Paul declares, "We know that in all things God works for the good of those who love Him, who have been called according to His purpose" (Rom. 8:28).

NINE

"This book is primarily concerned with the Day of Yahweh. . . . God's judgment was imminent. . . . The prophet, however, is not a pessimist. Beyond the impending doom he sees a better day. God must bring His people through the afflicting fires in order to prepare them to be a means of blessing to all mankind" (J.D. Douglas, ed., THE NEW BIBLE DICTIONARY, IVP, p. 1358).

"Zephaniah, speaking under the inspiration of the Spirit, and perfectly understanding that the outward appearance of reform was not indicative of a true change of heart, ignored it. He declared the terrors of divine judgment against sin. Yet to him fell the lot of uttering the very sweetest lovesong in the Old Testament" (G. Campbell Morgan, THE ANALYZED BIBLE, F.H. Revell, p. 329).

"His complaint is almost wholly against the privileged classes, the rich and the powerful; yet he does not pose as the spokesman of the poor and there is lacking in his utterances that note of sympathy with their sufferings which is so evident in Amos and Micah, a lack easily explained if he himself were a member of the aristocracy and had never felt the pinch of poverty" (J.M.P. Smith, MICAH, ZEPHANIAH, NAHUM, HABAKKUK, OBADIAH, JOEL, Charles Scribner's Sons, p. 177).

"He first denounces utter destruction on a people who were so perverse. . . . He afterwards turns his discourse to the faithful, and exhorts them to patience, setting before them the hope of favor, provided they ever looked to the Lord" (John Calvin, COMMENTARIES ON THE MINOR PROPHETS, Calvin Translation Society, vol. 4, p. 181).

ZEPHANIAH ULTIMATE ISSUES

THE INTRODUCTION to this prophecy is brief, but significant:

> The word of the Lord that came to Zephaniah son of Cushi, the son of Gedaliah, the son of Amariah, the son of Hezekiah, during the reign of Josiah son of Amon king of Judah (Zeph. 1:1).

And what, exactly, is so important about these words? Simply stated, to understand the role of Zephaniah, we need to know more about Amon and Josiah; for this prophet did not speak in a vacuum, but in a context influenced by the social, political, economic, and religious developments of the dark age in which he lived.

Amon was the son of Manasseh, whose reign in Jerusalem was as wicked as it was long. From 697 to 642 B.C., Manasseh presided over a period of religious decline. Afraid of the Assyrians and yet fascinated by their cults, he encouraged the worship of false gods in Judah and adulterated the worship of Jehovah. Under his misguided rule, illegal altars were placed in the Lord's temple courts and spiritism, sorcery, and the worship of the stars flourished. Manasseh consulted with mediums, practiced the cult of the dead, and even subjected his own son to the pagan ritual of passing through fire. He did evil in the eyes of the Lord and followed the detestable ways of the heathen. As a result, Manasseh kindled the anger of a holy and righteous God, and caused His wrath to hover over the land of Judah (2 Kings 21:1-18).

When Manasseh died, his twenty-two-year-old son, Amon, became king. Concerning him, we read:

> He did evil in the eyes of the Lord, as his father Manasseh had done. He walked in all the ways of his father; he worshiped the idols his father had worshiped, and bowed down to them. He forsook the Lord . . . and did not walk in the way of the Lord (2 Kings 21:20-22).

Within two years, Amon was murdered by some of his own palace officials. Then "the people of the land" brought the conspirators to justice and made Josiah, son of Amon, king in his place (2 Kings 21:23-24).

Josiah was only eight years of age when he became king in 640 B.C., but "he did what was right in the eyes of the Lord" (2 Kings 22:1-2). He was eager to see Judah and Jerusalem purged of idols and altars to strange gods, and he wished to repair the temple of the Lord his God (2 Chron. 34:1-8). Zephaniah first enters this picture as one who encourages Josiah's reforming efforts. Yet the prophet soon comes to realize that the newfound piety of the people of Judah is only shallow and temporary. Initial efforts at reform will not prove radical enough to avert God's coming judgment on this sinful race. And so, inspired by the Lord, he begins to prophesy.

Zephaniah's rough rhetoric is no more popular today than when it first thundered out and resounded in the consciences of his contemporaries. But what we have here is not cynical invective. It is inspired prophecy, vibrant with the very authority of the living God who is displeased and disgusted by the world's apparently inexorable descent into moral emptiness and confusion.

In an age of rebellion and apostasy, when idolatry, immorality, and pseudo-intellectual skepticism proliferated like malignant weeds, God raised up Zephaniah to speak His truth and uproot evil. Zephaniah's message—delivered with courage and earnestness twenty-six centuries ago—is timeless and, therefore, timely. Through this authentic spokesman—who communicates in language that is austere and often agonizing—the Lord makes us aware of two of life's ultimate issues: retribution and redemption.

(1) Day of Retribution
    A. On Judah (1:1-18)
    B. On Pagan Nations (2:4-15)
    C. On Jerusalem (3:1-8)

(2) Day of Redemption
    A. Contrition (2:1-3)
    B. Purification (2:6-7; 3:9-13)
    C. Celebration (3:14-20)

DAY OF RETRIBUTION

On Judah. The prophet explains that the Lord threatens to sweep away everything contaminated by the deadly virus of sin (1:2-3). He will take action against Judah. Not even Jerusalem will be spared. God will cut off every last vestige of the worship of Baal, Molech, and the starry host. The Lord's anger is kindled by those who try to serve both the living God *and* the idols of the heathen. He detests this adulteration of true worship. He hates a divided allegiance and will punish the sin of syncretism severely (1:4-6).

Zephaniah's point is clear: It is evil to abandon the worship of God. It also is sinful to combine the worship of the true God with devotion to the false gods of this world—such as power, pleasure, money, a political party, or the state. Our Lord puts it plainly:

You shall have no other gods before (besides) Me (Ex. 20:3).

No one can serve two masters. Either he will hate the one and love the other, or he will be devoted to the one and despise the other. You cannot serve both (Matt. 6:24).

The day of the sovereign Lord is drawing near, Zephaniah explains. On the altar of His justice. He will punish the ignoble nobility for its crimes (Zeph. 1:7-8). He will punish those who practice deceit and violence (1:9).

When the Lord judges Judah, He will do so discriminately; the innocent will not be punished. His judgment is accurate. But searching the land with a lamp that dispels the darkness, discovering the guilty with unfailing precision, He will punish those who have been complacent in their false security, those who have wrongly imagined that God is indifferent to what they do or fail to do. Their cynicism and skepticism will be utterly shattered on the day of judgment (1:10-13).

The great Day of the Lord is coming, the prophet announces (1:14). No one will be able to hold back the dawning of that awesome day. Zephaniah predicts:

> That day will be a day of wrath,
> a day of distress and anguish,
> a day of trouble and ruin,
> a day of darkness and gloom,
> a day of clouds and blackness (1:15).

This powerful prophecy has stirred the imagination of preachers and poets down through the centuries. Thomas of Celano (1190-1260), a Franciscan monk who lived in central Italy, wrote a hymn whose starting point was taken from this portion of Zephaniah's prophecy. It is known as the *Dies Irae* ("Day of Wrath") from the opening words of the Latin original.

Beginning with Zephaniah's prophetic statement, Thomas' hymn continues with an exposition of the dread theme of doom. Combining the rhythm of classical and medieval Latin, it deals with a sublime subject in simple language. He portrays the final collapse of the universe, the commotion of opening graves, the archangel with his trumpet, and the enthroned King of tremendous majesty who will judge everyone.

More than 100 translations of this hymn have been made. Woven into the texture of the *Mass for the Dead*, it also has been set to music by Mozart, Haydn, Berlioz, and Rachmaninoff. Something of its power and intensity come to us in Sir Walter Scott's version, who renders three of Thomas' eighteen original verses like this:

That day of wrath, that dreadful day,
When heaven and earth shall pass away,
What power shall be the sinner's stay?
How shall he meet that dreadful day?

When shrivelling like a parched scroll,
The flaming heavens together roll;
When, louder yet, and yet more dread,
Swells the high trump that wakes the dead—

O, on that day, that wrathful day,
When man to judgment wakes from clay,
Be Thou the trembling sinner's stay,
Though heaven and earth shall pass away!

As in previous prophetic messages we've studied, we again can see that the revelation of God's wrath is not the arbitrary action of some capricious divinity determined to vent its spleen, nor an irrational vindictiveness directed against the innocent. It is the response of God's holy character to man's sin. When He sits in judgment, neither silver nor gold shall save the impenitent from the outpouring of His anger (Zeph. 1:17-18).

On Pagan Nations. The Lord who is the God of Abraham, Isaac, and Jacob is not a deity whose authority is limited to one locality. He is sovereign over all the nations of the earth, and none of the world's inhabitants are exempt from the administration of His justice.

Accordingly, He pronounces judgment against Gaza, Ashkelon, Ashdod, and Ekron. Canaan, land of the Philistines, is not spared from the manifestation of God's holy wrath (2:4-7). Moab and Ammon will be punished and suffer irreparable loss when the Lord destroys them and their idols (2:8-11). Ethiopia and Assyria—even mighty Nineveh, the capital of Assyria—will experience devastation and desolation (2:12-15).

Nations to the north, south, east, and west of Judah will be judged. God's jurisdiction has "combined far and near and all the points of the compass, i.e., universality" (H.L. Ellison, *The Old Testament Prophets*, Zondervan, p. 68). God is the judge of *all* the earth, and we all must appear before His judgment throne.

It also is important to notice that Zephaniah mentions that the nations will be punished for having insulted and mocked the Lord's people (2:10). When the Son of man comes in His glory, enthroned to judge the nations, He will separate the sheep from the goats. Some will enter the kingdom of life, while others will be sent away into the realm of everlasting lostness. And the criterion of judgment He will use will focus on how men treated or mistreated *His people.* The King shall say:

> Whatever you did for one of the least of these brothers of Mine, you did for Me. . . . Whatever you did not do for one of the least of these, you did not do for Me (Matt. 25:40, 45).

The Apostle Paul similarly assures the persecuted church:

> God's judgment is right. . . . God is just: He will pay back trouble to those who trouble you and give relief to you who are troubled. . . . When the Lord Jesus is revealed from heaven in blazing fire with His powerful angels (2 Thes. 1:5-7).

On Jerusalem. The city of Jerusalem also must face up to the reality of coming judgment. Why? The prophet's indictment is unambiguous:

● Jerusalem is a city of oppressors, rebellious and defiled, insolent and insubordinate, neither willing to trust God nor to seek His presence (Zeph. 3:1-2).
● Jerusalem's officials are beasts of prey; her prophets are arrogant and treacherous; her priests profane the sanctuary and violate the Law. Princes, prophets, and priests stand in stark contrast to the Lord who is righteous and does no wrong (3:3-5).
● Jerusalem has persisted in the very sins that led to its downfall (3:6-7).

Having already predicted God's judgment against those who corrupt worship, Zephaniah now condemns injustice in the social order. The Lord will judge Judah and Jerusalem, the nations and the kingdoms, for this crime when His wrath is poured out on them all (3:8).

DAY OF REDEMPTION

Is there no way out of this predicted predicament? Fortunately, Zephaniah declares that we have more than a flicker of hope in the midst of the gathering darkness.

Contrition. Before the appointed time for judgment arrives, Zephaniah says, before the chaff is swept away and the fierce anger of the Lord is revealed, let sinners turn to God with contrite hearts:

> Seek the Lord, all you humble of the land, you who do what He commands. Seek righteousness, seek humility; perhaps you will be sheltered on the day of the Lord's anger (2:3).

This call to repentance is a vibrant echo of Isaiah 55:6-7, and is amplified by the apostles in the New Testament (Acts 2:38; 17:31; 2 Cor. 6:2; Heb. 3:6; 4:5). The truth of this message, though, is the same: If we draw near to God, then He will draw near to us (James 4:8).

Purification. The majority of the condemned people may refuse to repent, but a remnant—a minority—will truly turn from their sins. That remnant of the house of Judah will be blessed with Jehovah's pastoral care and the restoration of their fortunes (Zeph. 2:6-7).

The Lord will purify the lips of men and women, that they may call on Him with sincerity and truth. In partnership, they shall serve Him as the one true God (3:9). Purged of pride, the people will bring offerings to Him and humbly submit to His majesty. The meek and lowly, trusting in the Lord, will do what is right. They will speak no lies, practice no deceit, and enjoy genuine security (3:10-13).

The very virtues Zephaniah lists in his description of the purified remnant also are commended by Jesus in the Sermon on the Mount:

Blessed are the meek, for they will inherit the earth. Blessed are those who hunger and thirst for righteousness. ... Blessed are the pure in heart. ... Blessed are the peacemakers (Matt. 5:5-6, 8-9).

Celebration. Therefore, announces the prophet, since the Lord will accept the contrite remnant and purify His people, let the redeemed rejoice. Let the true Israel be glad, for the Lord has taken away its punishment and turned back its foes (Zeph. 3:14-15). The secret of joy and security is found in the presence of the King who dwells among His people and is mighty to save (3:16-17). This heartwarming reality inspires praise. God's final action is not one of wrath, but of grace:

He will quiet you with His love, He will rejoice over you with singing (3:17).

In effect, the Lord

... Embraces and cherishes His church, as a husband his wife whom he most tenderly loves. Such feelings, we know, belong not to God; but this mode of speaking, which often occurs in Scripture, is thus to be understood by us; for as God cannot otherwise show His favor towards us and the greatness of His love, He compares Himself to a husband, and us to a wife. ... God is most highly pleased when He can show Himself kind to His church (John Calvin, *Commentaries on the Minor Prophets*, Calvin Translation Society, vol. 4, p. 303).

The Lord will cause sorrow and sighing to flee away. He will release His people from all oppression, and gather home the scattered. Shame will give way to honor, and misery to prosperity (Zeph. 3:18-20). The prophet's predictions thus

... Point on directly to the blessed goal, and depict the Lord's dwelling in His church with mysterious fervor, His rule over the nations, with the extension of His church to all, so that differences of language and creed are abolished, and all as with one mouth call on His name, while His elect church is raised above every gulf separating it from the holy God (C. Von Orelli, *The Twelve Minor Prophets*, T. & T. Clark, p. 280).

What does this aspect of Zephaniah's prophecy mean for us as individuals? In the day of our final redemption, the Lord will rejoice over us. Having delivered us from the penalty and power of sin, He also will set us free from the very presence of sin. Even death, our last enemy, will be destroyed in the victory of life.

This sure and certain hope can help us endure difficulties and resist temptations. We can look beyond times of discipline to that final liberation. The revelation of Him who is Judge of all the earth is also the appearing of our Redeemer.

TEN

"No prophet ever appeared at a more critical juncture in the history of the people, and no prophet was more immediately successful" (Marcus Dods, HAGGAI, ZECHARIAH, MALACHI, T. & T. Clark, p. 44).

"Haggai is employed partly to reprove [Israel's] following their own interests, and neglecting the work of God, and to stir up that secure people to the work; partly to encourage them to go on, and to do it honestly being set about it" (George Hutcheson, A BRIEF EXPOSITION OF THE TWELVE SMALL PROPHETS, Ralph Smith, p. 315).

"Haggai came to confront the dangerous state of moral paralysis which accepts as normal conditions that demand drastic changes. Unless men of vision and determination can intervene in time there is no hope of recovery.... Half-hearted allegiance is no allegiance. To think that any time will do to become serious about His cause is to fail Him completely. He is waiting to bless, but He cannot do so while His people are apathetic and self-centered.... Haggai's remedy for today, as for his own day, is a church mobilized for action, to which he would say, 'Take courage, work, fear not!' God's purpose will be achieved and will prove to be more glorious in fulfillment than in prospect by the degree to which Jesus Christ was more glorious than the Temple" (Joyce Baldwin, HAGGAI, ZECHARIAH, MALACHI, Tyndale, pp. 27, 55).

HAGGAI CONSIDER YOUR WAYS

GIROLAMO SAVONAROLA was a powerful preacher in Renaissance Florence. He brooded about the plight of the world, worried about the decline of spiritual life, and preached that apocalyptic judgment was a prelude to spiritual renewal. Using rich imagery, expounding the Old Testament prophets, he evoked tears and terrors. Crowds came to the city's cathedral not to marvel at Giotto's graceful bell tower or Brunelleschi's grand dome, but to hear Savonarola's denunciations of political tyranny and ecclesiastical vice.

In November 1494, he began a series of sermons based on the prophecy of Haggai. Savonarola summoned listeners to repentance, warning that God would send plagues and allow the plunder of war if His urgent call was stubbornly disregarded. He pleaded for an end to the oppression of civil rulers, demanded amnesty for political prisoners, warned the insensitive rich, exposed merchants who inflated prices, and demanded bread for the hungry. He challenged the churches to melt down golden crosses and chalices, and to give the proceeds from the sale of precious metals to help the poor.

After four tumultuous years, Savonarola's voice finally was silenced. The same clerics whom he had denounced for their worldliness conspired to kill him. He was hanged as a heretic, his body burned, his ashes thrown into the Arno River.

In contrast to the fall of 1494, the summer of 520 B.C. was a very good season for authentic prophecy. God sent His people such spokesmen as Zechariah and Haggai, and the latter of these two delivered four prophetic messages, each of which is precisely dated:

In the second year of King Darius (520 B.C.) (1:1-15).

On the twenty-first day of the seventh month (2:1-9).

On the twenty-fourth day of the ninth month, in the second year of Darius (2:10-19).

On the twenty-fourth day of the month (2:20-23).

In addition to identifying exactly *when* he delivered his prophecies, Haggai repeatedly affirms *who* gave him his revelations. Over and over again, the prophet indicates, "then the word of the Lord came," or, "this is what the Lord Almighty says."

The contents of Haggai's prophecy may be considered under these headings:

(1) **One Assignment**
    A. Time to Build (1:2-8; 2:1-4)
    B. What to Build (1:2-4; 2:1-4)

(2) **Two Assertions**
    A. Negligence Means Loss (1:6-7, 9-11)
    B. Diligence Means Gain (1:8; 2:5, 8-9; 2:15-19)

(3) **Three Assurances**
    A. Divine Presence (1:12-14; 2:4-5)
    B. Messianic Hope (2:6-9)
    C. Final Victory (2:20-23)

ONE ASSIGNMENT

Though the word of the Lord came to the Prophet Haggai at various times during the second year of Darius' reign, and was addressed to persons long since vanished from the face of the earth, that word still is alive and powerful as it reaches us today. What the Lord had to say to Zerubbabel, the governor of Judah, and Joshua, the high priest, is still relevant to our situation in this time and place. Basically, Haggai tells us to get our priorities straight.

Time to Build. After the Babylonian Exile, when Cyrus gave the Israelites permission to return home and restore their ruined land (536 B.C.), the people immediately started to rebuild the temple in Jerusalem. This work, however, soon began to slow down. Eventually, it stopped completely. For more than a decade, in fact, nothing constructive happened. The people rationalized, "The time has not yet come for the Lord's house to be built" (Hag. 1:2).

In truth, the interest, resources, and efforts of the people of Judah had been diverted to other pursuits. Preoccupied with their own affairs, they had put God's project on the back burner. They had other priorities, and so the rebuilding of the temple was sadly neglected.

King David once told Nathan the prophet, "Here I am, living in a palace of cedar, while the ark of God remains in a tent" (2 Sam. 7:2). David desired to build a suitable house for the ark and the worship of God. Similarly, the current residents of Judah dwelt in paneled houses while the Lord's house remained a ruin (Hag. 1:4). Unfortunately, they did not share David's constructive desire.

The Israelites, therefore, continued to stall. They recalled the temple in its former glory and compared that magnificent structure with the incomplete one before their eyes. They could never build as fine a temple again, they concluded, so why even bother? (2:3) By glamorizing "the good old days," though, they were missing the blessings and challenges of the present moment; they failed to face the future with genuine optimism.

Recognizing Israel's true motivation, Haggai declares that the people and their leaders must now give themselves anew to the work of rebuilding the temple:

> This is what the Lord Almighty says: "Give careful thought to your ways. Go up into the mountains and bring down timber and build the house, so that I may take pleasure in

it and be honored," says the Lord (1:7-8).

The prophet's challenge comes particularly to Zerubbabel, governor of Judah, and to Joshua, the high priest. Together with the people, they are to channel their energies and resources into the rebuilding of God's house (2:1-4).

What to Build. It is evident from what we already have noted that the main issue Haggai is addressing concerns the restoration of the temple (1:2-4; 2:1-4). So what does this message have to do with us? We're not exiles who have returned from Babylon. We're not confronted with the ruins of a temple in Jerusalem. Does the exhortation of Haggai have any relevance to us today?

At the very least, the word of Haggai means that we shouldn't be satisfied with worshiping in dilapidated church buildings if we're living in comfortable high-rise apartments, suburban split-levels, or rural homes that abound in big city conveniences. Without giving in to an "edifice complex"— which erects extravagant structures and leaves a congregation in debt for decades to come—we should have facilities of dignity and beauty for the worship of God.

But Haggai's message clearly goes beyond this. The temple of God, in the New Testament, refers to God's people. Like living stones drawn from many cultural quarries, they are built on the firm foundation of the apostles and prophets, with Jesus Christ as the unifying cornerstone. The Lord's own are to become a sanctuary for the indwelling Spirit of God (Eph. 2:20-22; 1 Peter 2:5). Through evangelistic outreach, new stones are added and the temple takes shape. Through education, nurture, and fellowship, we learn how to fit in with one another as mutually supportive members of the true church.

We should understand Haggai's call as our summons to build up the church. This is done as we edify one another in love. What good is it to construct a house of worship in Romanesque, Gothic, or Georgian style, if we fail to build up *people?*

The Apostle Paul emphasized the importance of mutual edification when he wrote about each believer doing his or her part to further the spiritual maturity of others. When that happens, the Apostle said, we no longer will be infants, tossed back and forth by the winds and waves of false doctrine. Instead, speaking the truth in love, we will further our progress in godliness under the unique headship of Christ. From Him, the entire body draws vitality and so builds itself up in love as each member functions properly (Eph. 4:12-16).

Jude, the brother of our Lord, similarly challenges us to live in a way that differs radically from the death-style of those who are unspiritual and divisive. He tells us plainly,

> Build yourselves up in your most holy faith and pray in the Holy Spirit. Keep yourselves in God's love as you wait for the mercy of our Lord Jesus Christ to bring you to eternal life (Jude 20-21).

Do we hear what the Spirit is saying to us through Haggai? Are we doing something constructive to build up people and rebuild the church? However much we may need places of worship, generous funding, and efficient administration, we simply *must* have more people-builders.

Joses, better known as Barnabas, was a wonderful people-builder during the early days of the church. As the Book of Acts notes, he gave willingly for the support of the poor; sponsored a new convert named Saul of Tarsus when others treated him with fear or suspicion; encouraged the young disciples at Syrian Antioch to persevere; encouraged Paul in his first missionary journey; followed a course of conciliation when others pushed for confrontation; and gave John Mark a second chance to prove himself after shameful failure. Barnabas edified churches because he built up *people*. We may have the buildings, the boards, and the budgets, but where are the sons and daughters of Barnabas?

John Knox applied Haggai's exhortation to the rebuilding of the church in Scotland during the sixteenth century. Appropriately known as "The Thundering Scot," Knox vigorously expounded the message of Haggai to call the people to share in the work of restoring the Scottish Kirk. Whenever the Lord's spiritual temple is desecrated by heresy, schism, or immorality, Haggai's call to reconstruction is always relevant (1 Cor. 3:16-17).

TWO ASSERTIONS

The Lord's command to Zerubbabel and Joshua is clear: Be strong and get on with the work. This command, however, also is addressed to all the people of the land. The project cannot be treated as the exclusive concern of "the clergy," with "the laity" involved only as peripheral spectators.

Negligence Means Loss. To motivate the leaders and people to work together to rebuild the temple, the Lord reminds Israel of the consequences of neglecting this common task. The people have diverted their time, energy, and resources from the rebuilding of the temple to other pursuits. Therefore, God has withheld blessing from them. They have sown much, but harvested little. They eat, but still are hungry. No drinking can quench their thirst. They dress themselves fashionably, but still lack comfort. They try to save something from their wages, only to find this effort at thrift an exercise in futility (Hag. 1:6-7).

What they sought to hoard, God scattered by the breath of His wrath. The heavens sent down no dew to refresh the fields. Drought struck the land, affecting the harvest of corn, grapes, and olives. The labor of their hands led only to frustration, as God demonstrated His displeasure over their disordered priorities (1:9-11). This remembrance should serve as a negative encouragement for Israel. Such chastisement can only be averted through obedience. Doesn't it make sense, Haggai implies, to do things God's way?

Diligence Brings Gain. If negligence results in frustration and failure, diligence brings gain. Let the leaders and people of Judah set their hearts and hands to the task of reconstruction, the prophet proclaims, encouraged by the promises of God. The Lord Almighty takes pleasure in the obedience of His people and is honored by it (1:8). If they do their part, He certainly will do His and prove faithful to all with whom He covenanted at the time of the Exodus from Egypt (2:5).

When the people realize that the silver and gold they possess really belongs to the Lord, and they see themselves as stewards or trustees of His gifts, they will dedicate their resources to the work of reconstruction (2:8). Then will "the glory of this present house be greater than the glory of the former house" (2:9).

In contrast to the discipline and chastisement of disobedience, the Lord promises to bless His people richly as their penitent zeal finds expression in the restoration of His temple. Instead of blight, mildew, and hail, the blessing of an abundant harvest will be reaped (2:15-19).

Haggai's message must be heard, believed, and obeyed. The prophet insists that we get our priorities straight. In short, he is saying:

> Put first things first, and other things also necessary ... will follow as a result. Priority number one in human life is God, for to trust and to love, to revere and to worship, to obey and to serve Him, is the chief end of man (S.F. Winward, *A Guide to the Prophets*, Hodder & Stoughton, p. 195).

Our Lord echoes and amplifies the word of His servant Haggai by saying:

> Seek first His kingdom and His righteousness, and all these things will be given to you as well (Matt. 6:33).

THREE ASSURANCES

Haggai communicates three great messages of assurance to encourage everyone who answers God's call to constructive effort.

The Divine Presence. As Zerubbabel and Joshua lead the people in the task of rebuilding the temple, Haggai gives them this assurance from the Lord: "I am with you" (Hag. 1:13). The presence of God works to stir up the spirit of leaders and people alike, so that they can participate in the project enthusiastically.

Again, the Lord who exhorts the builders to be strong actually strengthens them with His presence. He says, "Be strong ... and work. For I am with you" (2:4). Moreover, the Lord says: "My Spirit remains among you. Do not fear" (2:5).

For us today, the presence of God gives us strength and courage in the enterprises to which we are called. As He entrusts us with the work of discipling the nations, He also gives us this blessed assurance: "Surely I will be with you always, to the very end of the age" (Matt. 28:20). We are not sent out alone.

The Messianic Hope. God's work will be accomplished. He will shake the heavens and the earth, the sea and the dry land, in the process of fulfilling His plan. Then, at the right moment, "The desired of all nations" will come. Then the Lord Almighty will fill His temple with glory (Hag. 2:6-7) and an abundance of peace (2:9).

The sovereign God even achieves His purpose in the rise and fall of political powers and through economic factors. He humbled Egypt at the time of Israel's deliverance and broke the Babylonian yoke to bring about the people's return from exile. But all such actions are only a prelude to the spreading of His kingdom. As Calvin notes, "When Christ shall be manifested, in whom the wishes of all ought to center, the glory of the second temple shall then be illustrious" (John Calvin, *Commentaries on the Minor Prophets*, Calvin Translation Society, vol. 4, p. 360). Indeed, Christ Himself will be the temple in whom God's glory will fully dwell (John 1:14; 2:19-22; Col. 2:9).

The Final Victory. Haggai delivers the word of the Lord to Zerubbabel to assure him that forces which are hostile to God's purpose shall not prevail. The Lord will "overturn royal thrones and shatter the power of the foreign kingdoms" in the process of manifesting the reality of His own authority (Hag. 2:20-22). The Lord also promises to honor Zerubbabel, His faithful servant, His chosen one, making him "like my signet ring" (2:23). What exactly does this phrase mean?

The signet or seal was:

A precious stone on which was engraved the name or some identifying emblem of the owner. The signet was impressed on soft clay tablets. . . . If papyrus or parchment was used, the seal was imprinted on wax or clay discs affixed to the documents (Theodore Laetsch, *The Minor Prophets*, Concordia, p. 401).

The signet verified the authenticity of the document and thus was highly valued.

Zerubbabel, then, was prized like a treasured signet. In fact, he became a link in the chain of ancestry between David and the coming Messiah (Matt. 1:12; Luke 3:27). In the fullness of time, Jesus Christ was born to be King of an everlasting kingdom (Luke 1:26-33). The Lord who speaks through His servants, the prophets, always keeps His word!

ELEVEN

"He propounds divers visions for the encouragement of that people in their low condition, and to go on in the work they had begun. . . . He comes to prophesie of the ruine of all their enemies round about, of the coming of Christ His death and passion, the pouring out of His Spirit, and the spreading of the Gospel, with the rejection of the Nation of the Jewes till the time appointed for their Conversion" (George Hutcheson, A Brief Exposition on the Twelve Small Prophets, Ralph Smith, p. 332).

"When the prophet looks forward to the future, and proclaims the purpose of the living God for the world, his vision includes not only men but things. Yes, right down to the very simplest things— the bells of the horses, the little, tinkling metal plates that were fastened to the headstall of the horses' harness" (A.A. Van Ruler, Zechariah Speaks Today, Lutterworth, p. 75).

"Zechariah serves to encourage the nation in its divinely appointed task. The indignation of the Lord has come . . . because of the people's sin. If the nation will humble itself before God, it will have a glorious future. . . . These future spiritual blessings will be brought about through the Messiah" (E.J. Young, An Introduction to the Old Testament, Eerdmans, pp. 300-301).

ZECHARIAH QUINTESSENCE OF THE PROPHETS

MARTIN LUTHER once called the Book of Zechariah "the quintessence of the prophets," for in it we find the essential nature of biblical prophecy. Here in the longest of the minor prophets, we discover visions and verbal communication from an authentic spokesman for the living God.

Despite Luther's glowing endorsement, the Book of Zechariah has remained, in some ways, the most obscure of the prophets. It arguably is one of the least known in the church today, and a veritable halo of mystery surrounds its author's head. Even when the book is mentioned, it usually finds itself in the center of critical arguments and speculations, as some scholars are convinced it is the product of multiple authorship.

For reasons shortly to be explained, I am convinced that Zechariah was the author of the entire prophecy; I also believe it is possible to dispel a good deal of the ambiguity enshrouding this most interesting prophet and his message.

The name, Zechariah, means "the Lord remembers," and at least thirty different people bear this name in the Scriptures. The author of this prophetic book, however, is identified solely as the son of Berekhiah, the grandson of Iddo. Zechariah began his prophetic ministry during the eighth month of the second year of the Persian king, Darius. He was a contemporary of Haggai—who began to deliver messages from God in the late summer of 520 B.C.—and he started to prophesy in the autumn of that same year.

Like Haggai, Zechariah was concerned over the discouragement of those who had returned from the Babylonian Captivity. The work of restoring Jerusalem to its former grandeur had yet to be completed. The temple still was a blackened ruin awaiting reconstruction. Zechariah therefore addressed himself to this situation, exhorting and encouraging the people of God in the great work of rebuilding.

His prophecy can best be viewed, I suggest, by considering its four messages:

(1) A Mysterious Message
   Zechariah's Visions (1:2-21; 2:1—6:15)

(2) A Messianic Message
   A. Messiah Revealed (9:9-10)
   B. Messiah Rejected (10:3; 11:11-17; 13:7)
   C. Messiah Rewarded (6:9-15)

(3) A Merciful Message
   A. A Sinful People (1:2-5; 7:11-14; 8:16-19)
   B. A Merciful God (3:1-10; 5:5-11; 12:10-14; 13:1)

(4) A Missionary Message
   A. The City of God (2:1-5, 10-13; 8:1-9; 13:9)
   B. The Glory of God (14:9, 16, 20-22)

A MYSTERIOUS MESSAGE

The Book of Zechariah is filled with night visions and enigmatic statements. It abounds in fascinating figurative language; an aura of mystery surrounds its words.

However, a clear call for repentance *is* made at the very outset of this book. The Lord summons the people to return to Him and promises to welcome all who respond penitently. Those who return will show their sincerity by breaking with evil practices and listening to God's voice. A failure to repent will result in ruin (1:2-6).

Zechariah then records a series of strange night visions. The prophet first sees a man riding a red horse, standing among myrtle trees in a ravine; red, brown, and white horses stand in the background (1:7-17). He also sees four horns and four craftsmen (1:18-21). He then beholds a man with a measuring line in his hand, going out to survey the length and breadth of the city of Jerusalem (2:1-13).

Next, the high priest appears in the Lord's presence, but he is clothed in filthy garments that disqualify him for the service of God (3:1-10). Then the prophet sees a seven-branched candlestick of solid gold. It has a bowl at the top, with seven lights on it. There are seven channels running from the bowl to the lights. There also are two olive trees, one on either side of the bowl, supplying it with oil for burning and brightness (4:1-14).

The prophet next sees a flying scroll, measuring thirty feet in length and fifteen feet in width (5:1-4). Then he describes a basket with a lid of lead, and a vision of women with wings, all suspended between heaven and earth (5:5-11).

Zechariah beholds four chariots coming out from between two mountains of bronze. Each of these chariots is drawn by powerful horses colored red, black, white, and dappled. They are straining to run throughout the whole earth (6:1-8). Finally, the seer contemplates crowns of silver and gold (6:9-15).

What exactly do these fascinating figures of speech mean? How shall we interpret them? Unfortunately, a detailed consideration of each of these visions is prevented by the space limitations of this book. But such passages clearly deserve concentrated, consecrated study; we therefore should draw on biblical commentaries by such scholars as Calvin, Keil, Moore, and Unger for more detailed treatments.

In this book, we *will* review several of these visions and note their significance where appropriate. However, one word of caution should be sounded at this point. We need to be careful that in studying Zechariah's complex and speculative elements, we don't miss the great simplicities and centralities of his prophecy.

We must never forget that all of Scripture—including Zechariah—is given by divine inspiration for two major purposes: first, to lead us to a saving faith in Jesus Christ; second, to prepare us for living obediently for His honor and glory

(2 Tim. 3:14-17). Both of these purposes are realized in Zechariah's prophetic message.

A MESSIANIC MESSAGE

During the 1960s, it was my privilege to pastor Philadelphia's Tenth Presbyterian Church. My family and I lived in the center of the city, near Rittenhouse Square. One evening, at suppertime, we heard over the radio that a famous person was making a surprise visit to our city; his motorcade, in fact, would be passing within a few blocks of the manse. The streets already were filled with people by the time my younger son, Peter, and I arrived at the scene. In a few moments, the motorcade passed by and I lifted my son up so he could see above the crowd. It was there, a few days before his assassination, that we saw John F. Kennedy.

As I lifted my son up to see a passing President, so the prophets and apostles of the Bible help us behold Jesus the Messiah. Their words, written through the inspiration of the Holy Spirit, lift us up and encourage us to contemplate Christ and behold His glory with eyes of faith.

On the Emmaus road, our risen Lord enlightened and encouraged His followers by referring to the Scriptures of the Old Testament. He clearly showed how both His humiliation and exaltation had been predicted there. The prophets spoke of the sufferings and the glory of the Messiah. They prophesied about His cross and crown. To demonstrate this fact beyond all shadow of doubt, Jesus drew on Moses and the prophets as He explained what was said in all the Scriptures concerning Himself (Luke 24:25-27, 44-46).

We, therefore, have abundant warrant to interpret some of Zechariah's prophecies in terms of Christ. Indeed, such writers of the New Testament Gospels as Matthew and John did this very thing. They boldly related many events recorded in their Gospels to what was written by Zechariah the prophet.

Messiah Revealed. Consider, first, the revelation of the Messiah as covered in Zechariah. How does He appear on the scene of history? The prophet points out that He comes with gentleness and righteousness, to proclaim peace and bring salvation. Fierce foes may oppose Him, but the final victory is His. His rule shall extend over all. Therefore, let the people of this great King rejoice and sing out in praise to God because of Him (Zech. 9:9-10). We know that this prophecy was fulfilled on that first Palm Sunday, when Jesus entered Jerusalem and was acclaimed King (Matt. 21:4-5).

Messiah Rejected. Zechariah also prophesies about the shepherding role of the Messiah. Other pastors have mistreated God's flock, feeding themselves but fleecing the sheep, he says. They have plundered and abandoned the people. These false and dangerous demagogues have misled the people entrusted to their care. They are blind leaders of the blind (Matt. 15:14). Themselves deceived, they have deceived others. These merciless mercenaries will experience God's judgment (Zech. 10:3; 11:16-17).

Jesus, the Good Shepherd who has faithfully cared for the flock, who has tenderly cared for the bruised and the weak, will not be appreciated. Instead, Zechariah says, He will be despised and rejected by an unthinking people. When He puts them to the test by asking for His severance pay, they will not plead with Him to stay on as their shepherd. On the contrary, they actually will pay Him off with thirty pieces of silver. They will underestimate the value of His services and give Him the price paid for a gored animal or a mutilated slave (Zech. 11:11-13; Matt. 26:14-16).

As Zechariah 9:9-10 was fulfilled on that first Palm Sunday, so Zechariah 11:11-13 became history when Judas Iscariot betrayed Christ for thirty pieces of silver.

The prophet further describes the Messiah's humiliation and suffering when he says that the shepherd will be stricken and His sheep scattered. This is precisely what happened on the night of Jesus' betrayal and arrest (Zech. 13:7; Matt. 26:31).

Messiah Rewarded. If Zechariah prophesies of the coming and the cross of Christ, he also affirms the Messiah's coronation. The Shepherd who is despised and rejected of men, who is considered worth only thirty pieces of silver, who is arrested and stricken, deserted by his friends, and wounded by His foes, will also be crowned with glory and honor. His descent into the depths of humiliation will be followed by an ascent to the pinnacle of authority and power.

This development is symbolically portrayed in the passage

where Zechariah speaks of silver and gold being used to make a crown for the head of the High Priest. The One who is to be crowned possesses true humanity. He also is known as "the Branch," coming forth from the royal line of David's family tree. This King will build the Lord's temple. Clothed with majesty, He will accomplish the task entrusted to Him and rule on His everlasting throne (Zech. 6:9-15; Phil. 2:5-11; Heb. 1:1-3).

The One who is thus crowned and enthroned is no pitiless autocrat. He is the merciful High Priest who fully understands our infirmities (Heb. 4:14-16). He reconciles those who are both near and far. The secret of harmony with heaven, the secret of peace on earth, is to be found in commitment to Christ and submission to His unique Sovereignty (2 Cor. 5:18-21; Eph. 2:19-22; Col. 1:20).

A MERCIFUL MESSAGE

We must remember that the message of Zechariah originally was addressed to the inhabitants of Jerusalem. What sort of people were they? Can we identify with them in any way? How is the message first given to them also relevant to us?

A Sinful People. The people of Jerusalem were the product of an obstinate generation. Their forefathers had disobeyed God; they neither kept His covenant nor heeded His warnings. They impenitently persisted in the perverse path of disobedience. That is why they experienced the discipline of the Lord and were allowed to pass under the power of pagans in the Babylonian Captivity (Zech. 1:2-5; 7:11-14).

Zechariah's contemporaries were preoccupied with ritual observances rather than practical righteousness. When a delegation of religious leaders finally came to ask questions of this prophet, they spent most of their time inquiring about ceremonies! They wanted to know about regulations governing fasting! They weren't really interested in learning how to establish a right relationship with the Lord, or how to practice righteousness in their dealings with one another.

Zechariah makes it crystal clear that God's divine requirement goes far deeper than the superficial righteousness of external observance. Speaking for the Lord God Almighty, he declares:

Administer true justice; show mercy and compassion to one another. Do not oppress the widow or the fatherless, the alien or the poor. In your hearts do not think evil of each other (7:9-10).

These are the things you are to do: Speak the truth to each other, and render true and sound judgment in your courts; do not plot evil against your neighbor, and do not love to swear falsely.... Love truth and peace (8:16-19).

A Merciful God. The people to whom Zechariah brought the Word of the Lord needed cleansing from the pollution of sin. As we saw earlier, he mentions a symbolic description of the high priest—a person set apart for the service of God— who is clothed in filthy garments which render him unfit for divine service and open to the accusation of Satan. Nevertheless, God treats this priest with mercy. The sin-defiled garments are taken away. Fresh clothing is provided, so that the priest might now appear in the service of a holy God without shame and yield to Him a new obedience (3:1-10).

Surely, this is a marvelous portrayal of the biblical doctrine of justification by faith. We who are stained by sin, accused by Satan, and incapable of rendering acceptable service to the holy God can, nevertheless, experience acquittal and acceptance. The Apostle Paul says that our sin can be removed and our personality clothed in the robe of the righteousness of Christ (Phil. 3:9). When we put our trust in Jesus, the liability for our sin is transferred to Him who bears it away, and the assets of His unsearchable riches are credited to our account.

Zechariah says that the sin of the people will be removed from the land in a single day. Is this promise symbolized by that strange vision of a woman in a basket who is carried away by two other women with stork-like wings? (Zech. 5:5-11) If the woman in the basket under the leaden lid represents the sin of the people, then the message is this: When God forgives, He forgets. He bears away our sins, removing them as far from us as the east is from the west (Ps. 103:8-12; John 1:29).

The prophet further predicts that men and women will look on Him whom they have pierced and mourn because of Him.

This will come about as the Spirit of grace and supplication makes stony hearts sensitive to what sin did to the Messiah (Zech. 12:10-14). This prophecy found fulfillment at Calvary (John 19:37-38) and still is being fulfilled today as people recognize their sin and come to repentance (Acts 2:37-38). This prophecy also will be fulfilled when the day of grace is over; those whose transgressions pierced God's Son shall mourn as they face their irrevocable doom (Rev. 1:7).

In that day, when the Messiah dies for the sins of His people, a fountain will open for the cleansing of every guilty soul in the house of David and among the people of Jerusalem (Zech. 13:1). The New Testament tells us that the blood of Jesus Christ cleanses us from sin's pollution. We are spared from judgment, cleansed, and forgiven, because Another took our place and punishment. Jesus Christ is the sacrificial Lamb, the Just who dies for the unjust, atoning for our sins. Confessing our faults and confiding in this Saviour, we are purified and pardoned (1 John 1:7-9). Zechariah foretells this very truth.

A MISSIONARY MESSAGE
The City of God. The city of God, the prophet tells us, is meant to be a city without walls (Zech. 2:1-5). The reason for this will soon be apparent.

Of course, there is a sense in which the people of God *need* protective walls. Anything that is not in keeping with biblical standards of doctrine and morality must be excluded. The people of God are called to vigilance lest moral compromise and doctrinal defection infect the church.

Nevertheless, in another sense, the city of God must be *without* walls. The growth of the church, spreading from center to circumference, is consistent with the will of God (Zech. 2:1-5). Surely, this is reminiscent of our Lord's saying just prior to His ascension. Jesus declared that the disciples, in the power of the Holy Spirit, would become His witnesses. Starting at Jerusalem, moving into Judea and Samaria, and extending to the very ends of the earth, they would bring the Gospel of Christ to all nations (Acts 1:8).

What is the secret to this amazing growth of the city of God? The key is not found in some technique perfected by men, but in the presence of the living God. When He lives in the midst of His people, the church has vitality. When He guards His people, they are everlastingly secure (Zech. 2:5). Open to people of every kindred, language, culture, and nation on the face of the earth, the city will experience constant expansion and phenomenal growth (Zech. 2:10-13; Rev. 5:9).

God loves His people with an everlasting love, Zechariah continues. He will return and dwell among His people. Thus will Jerusalem become the City of Truth. Its citizens will experience length of life and a secure existence blessed with prosperity. The holy remnant will be restored and prospered. They will acknowledge the Lord as their God, and He will acknowledge them as His people. Together, they will observe and enjoy a covenant relationship (Zech. 8:1-9). The people will be strong because the Almighty is their God. They will call on His name with humble and total dependence. God will embrace them as His people, and they will rejoice in their allegiance to the Lord of the covenant (13:9).

The Glory of God. Zechariah promises that the Lord will overcome all His foes and ours. He will be recognized as King over the whole world. On that day, only one Lord and only one sacred name will be revered by all. His royal authority will manifest itself in the liberation of the oppressed and the condemnation of oppressors. Even the ordinary things of life—such as the bells fastened to a horse's harness and kitchen pots—will be thought of as consecrated to the service of God (Zech. 14:9, 16, 20-21).

Rather than running from the "secular" and taking refuge in "the sacred," Zechariah's prophecy tells us that we must dedicate every legitimate aspect of our daily life to the glory of the Lord. Redeemed by this Lord, we must give Him our willing allegiance and obedience—regardless of the way in which others ignore or defy His rule. We do not belong to ourselves but to Him who set us free, and we are committed to please Him in every lawful endeavor—whether in art, literature, science, business, education, politics, church relationships, or family life. The Redeemer's glory must always be our chief end and highest joy (1 Cor. 6:19-20; 10:31).

Johann Sebastian Bach used to dedicate his works to the glory of God. He knew that the cantatas and fugues he wrote were simply the expression of a talent received from God and dedicated to Him. But suppose your work is not as creative as Bach's. What then? Can it still be consecrated to a holy God? After all, isn't what you do to earn a living between Sundays purely a secular pursuit? Of course, ministers and missionaries are called to "full-time service" for God. But what about the rest of us?

Zechariah's prophecy envisions the consecration of the commonplace to the glory of God. All of life is to be lived in keeping with the Lord's standard of holiness. The Apostle Paul urges us to commit all our activities to God's glory. We are workers together with Him. He calls us to serve Him acceptably, whether we are preaching from a pulpit, counseling in a study, performing surgery in a hospital, or parenting at home.

The service we render to others, whether in church, state, factory, or family is to be done "for His sake." As George Herbert put it in his seventeenth-century hymn, "Teach Me, My God and My King":

> Teach me, my God and King.
> In all things Thee to see,
> And what I do in anything
> To do it as for Thee.
>
> A servant with this clause
> Makes drudgery divine;
> Who sweeps a room as for Thy laws
> Makes that an action fine.

We are to demonstrate the liberating power of the Gospel in the freedom and joy with which we do our daily work. Luther and Calvin underlined this biblical emphasis during the days of the Reformation. They understood that man's chief end was to glorify God in all of life's relationships and occupational or cultural pursuits. Our century, so secular and profane, needs to recover Zechariah's vision of total dedication to the Lord.

Zechariah's concluding words point toward the sublime close of the Apocalypse, in which the holiness of God's kingdom is portrayed so magnificently. As one commentator has summarized this vision:

> All shall be happy because all shall be holy. Sorrow shall cease because sin shall cease. The groaning earth shall be covered with joy because the trail of the serpent shall be gone, and the Eden of the future makes us cease to look back with longing at the Eden of the past (T.V. Moore, *Zechariah*, Banner of Truth Trust, pp. 236-237).

TWELVE

"Malachi breaks forth into the exalted language of prophecy in declaring that the messenger of the Lord will truly come and prepare the way for the Lord who will appear as a refiner, to purify and purge the nation" (J.D. Douglas, ed., THE NEW BIBLE DICTIONARY, IVP, p. 774).

"This prophet is raised up by God when the people's zeal was decayed, purity of worship corrupted, and vices had crept in amongst them, and all things were now growen worse. . . . The scope of the Prophecie is partly to reprove these grosse faults, partly to encourage the godly who kept their integrity in such declining times, and partly to foretell most distinctly the coming of Christ in the flesh" (George Hutcheson, A BRIEF EXPOSITION ON THE TWELVE SMALL PROPHETS, Ralph Smith, p. 405).

"More than other prophets, he unveils priests and people to themselves, interprets their thoughts to them, and puts those thoughts in abrupt naked language, picturing them as demurring to every charge which he brought against them. . . . Malachi is like a late evening, which closes a long day, but he is at the same time the morning twilight which bears in its bosom a glorious day . . . the rising beams of the Sun of Righteousness" (E.B. Pusey, THE MINOR PROPHETS, Funk & Wagnalls, p. 595).

"A fitting end to the prophetic books. It looks back to the revelation of God on which the whole prophetic message is based, and forward to the fulfillment of all the prophetic hopes" (H.L. Ellison, THE PROPHETS OF ISRAEL, Eerdmans, p. 136).

MALACHI
LAST BUT
NOT LEAST

IT HAPPENED IN THE SHADOW of a cathedral. My wife and I were touring the Italian city of Bari on the Adriatic and were looking forward to visiting the town's impressive Romanesque church. Yet as we admired the cathedral's beautiful outer facade—which features a large rose window surrounded by sculptured beasts and monsters—two men on a motorcycle raced past us. Before we realized what was happening, one of them snatched my wife's purse.

I immediately ran after them, screaming, "Robbers! Robbers!" but no one stopped them for fear of reprisal. They swiftly disappeared through the crowd in the square, and into one of several winding streets characteristic of the old town. Our travelers' checks, passports, keys, address books, notes on family birthdays and anniversaries—all were gone. Some things could be replaced, but others would remain only in our fading memories.

Robbery upsets us when the loss is our own. We want to see swift justice done. Let the police and courts of law do their work: apprehend the criminals, recover what has been stolen, pass sentence after due process, and impose deserved punishment!

But are we aware that we sometimes rob *God*? Malachi, a truly courageous prophet, makes this very charge—and others—against people who outwardly profess to be religious.

Malachi may be the last of the twelve minor prophets, but he certainly is not the least of them. There is nothing "minor" about his message. He directs his prophecy to people guilty of neglecting God's orders, as a spokesman for Him who is sure to deal with moral evil. Yet Malachi also speaks a refreshing word about the abundant blessings reserved for everyone who returns to the Lord and begins to do His will with a willing heart.

Like Haggai and Zechariah, Malachi was a prophet of the Restoration era. The Books of Ezra and Nehemiah record the historical events which transpired during the very time that these prophets spoke. Haggai and Zechariah began serving God's cause of reconstruction in 520 B.C., while Malachi came on the scene seventy-five years later, at the close of this period. Still, he had a distinctive message from the Lord for his contemporaries. And the same Spirit who inspired Malachi's writings can speak to us through those Scriptures today. Accordingly, we would do well to examine the content of this prophet's message.

In four brief chapters, punctuated by questions, affirmations, objections, precepts, and promises, Malachi delivers a message whose contemporary relevance is beyond all doubt. Its many facets can be considered under two main headings: a broken covenant (strained relationships) and a blessed advent (messianic expectations).

(1) **Broken Covenant**
    A. Estranged People (1:2-14; 2:17; 3:8-18)
    B. Ruined Marriages (2:10, 14-17)
    C. Faithless Priests (2:1-9)

(2) **Blessed Advent**
    A. Purpose of Advent (3:1-6; 4:1-2)
    B. Preparation for Advent (4:3-6)

BROKEN COVENANT

What is a covenant? This is an extremely important word; in fact, our faith is not really understandable apart from it. One scholar defines a covenant like this:

Basically, it denotes a compact or agreement between two parties binding them mutually to undertakings on each other's behalf. Theologically (used of relations between God and man) it denotes a gracious undertaking entered into by God for the benefit and blessing of man, and specifically of those men who by faith, receive the promises and commit themselves to the obligations which this undertaking involves (E.F. Harrison, ed., *Baker's Dictionary of Theology*, Baker, p. 142).

Covenants have an important place in biblical history. God made a covenant with Adam, promising him a certain type of life if he remained in perfect obedience to the Creator and did not partake of the forbidden fruit (Gen. 2:16-17). The Lord covenanted with Abraham. Isaac, Jacob, and their descendants (Gen. 6:18; 9:9-17; 17:1-8). He similarly acknowledged Israel as His people, promising to provide and protect them, while they were committed to trust and obey Him alone (Josh. 24:1-27).

Estranged People. In light of this special history, Malachi declares that Israel has strained its covenant relationship with God. The people have doubted, and even denied, the Lord's love toward them (Mal. 1:2-5). They have received benefits from His hand and yet responded with ingratitude. They claimed to be His children and heirs, but failed to honor Him as their Father. He is Lord, as the people's prayers sometimes confess, but His laws are continually disregarded.

In point of fact, Israel despises His sacred name and offers polluted bread on the altar. They treat His table with contempt. The people have wearied the Lord with their faulty thinking. They have imagined that God rewards evildoers and actually condones acts of injustice! (2:17)

And so they merely go through the ritual of religion while they reject the Lord of the temple. For this, God shall reject them. In His sovereign grace, He will turn to the heathen and offer the blessings of salvation to the pagan world (1:6-14).

Our Lord has said that it is far more blessed to give—overcoming our covetousness and helping others—than to receive and hoard (Acts 20:35). But Israel's estrangement from the God of the covenant is expressed by the fact that the people

fail to honor Him with their tithes and offerings (Mal. 3:8).
When it comes to giving, they feel smugly complacent about
the few crumbs they occasionally let fall from their tables to
support God's work. In so doing, Malachi says, they miss
God's promised blessing (3:9-12).

The estranged people also have said harsh things against
the Lord. They accuse *Him* of ignoring obedience and sacrifice, while rewarding the arrogant who do evil. Such slander
is most reprehensible (3:13-15). Malachi's denunciation of Israel's irreverence, ingratitude, and insolence is, therefore,
thoroughly justified. The people had wandered away from
God and stubbornly resisted His call to come home again.

While some individuals—in their cynicism and skepticism—charge God with being morally insensitive, there are
others who sincerely revere Him. The Lord knows these persons and treasures them. He will make it plain that He *does*
distinguish between the righteous and the wicked, between
those who serve God and those who don't (3:16-18).

Ruined Marriages. Malachi repeats his charge that the Israelites have failed to keep their covenant with God and with
each other. He accuses them of breaking their promises, leaving obligations unmet, and dealing treacherously out of self-
interest (2:10).

This is particularly true, he says, with respect to their marriage relationships. Broken promises, broken families, estrangement, alienation, divorce—all these actions displease
the God who has given us the gift of sexuality and who has
ordained marriage for the well-being and happiness of the
human race (2:14-17). The family is basic to the stability and
sanity of the social order. Anything that undermines it—
whether pornography, promiscuity, adultery, fornication,
emotional incompatibility, or financial irresponsibility—must
be recognized as destructive, decisively repudiated, and finally overcome by the grace of God.

Faithless Priests. The priests, who should show leadership
in the worship of God, are especially guilty of misleading
Israel and encouraging disrespect for the Lord. Speaking for
the Almighty, Malachi urges the priests to listen to him and
change their ways—or face fearful consequences. They ought
to take his message to heart and glorify God—while there is

still time. If they persist on the wrong road, the Lord will curse them with corruption and humiliation (2:1-3).

Malachi reminds the religious leaders of what God expects them to be. They should know His Law, teach it faithfully, and serve Him only. Yet they depart from the path of duty and lead others astray. They break the covenant through neglect and disobedience. God will expose their falsehood and deprive them of all moral authority (2:7-9).

In contrast to these reprehensible priests, Malachi portrays the messianic priest revealed in Jesus Christ. He is the One who keeps the covenant, is perfectly obedient to God, shows reverence and righteousness, restores peace between sinful men and the holy God, and brings life to His people (2:4-6).

CONTEMPORARY RELEVANCE

We should never assume that Malachi's prophecy has nothing to do with us. If we are professing Christians, we have entered into a covenant with God. We have publicly acknowledged our faith in the Father, the Son, and the Holy Spirit. We have promised to support the work and worship of the church, and to further its witness in the world. Many of us have taken vows to serve as pastors, elders, or deacons.

But, have we all been diligent in the reading and hearing of the Word, the practice of prayer, and the meaningful remembrance of the sacrifice symbolized in the Lord's Supper? How faithfully have we kept our marriage vows, or the promise to bring up our children in the nurture and admonition of the Lord? Are we guilty of a halfhearted devotion, a mere external observance of religious duties devoid of fervor and sincerity? Is our piety simply pretense? With what attitude do we draw near to God in public worship?

It is possible to go through our religious motions and feel nothing but monotony; to be jaded with the great realities of redemption; to take the wonder of the virgin birth, the atoning death, the mighty resurrection, and the glorious ascension of our Lord for granted. The perfunctory way in which some Christians recite the Apostles' Creed betrays a lack of passionate conviction and consuming zeal. So does the low level of giving characteristic of many in this age of affluence—whether it involves donating money, time, or skills for the furtherance of the Lord's work. Is it any wonder that boredom, rather than blessing, is the experience of those who "go to church" but fail to meet with the Lord?

When the Spirit speaks to us through the probing and penetrating words of the Prophet Malachi, our response should be one of penitence, instead of self-justification. Repentance is the first step back to the way of joy in the service of God.

Surely, this aspect of Malachi's message is timely. One of the greatest problems facing the church today is the faithlessness of some who have been ordained as ministers of the Word of God. They have taken their vows before bishops, conferences, presbyteries, and congregations—sometimes, though, with ecclesiastical tongue in ecclesiastical cheek. Professing to acknowledge the Bible as the written, inspired, and authoritative Word of God, they have proceeded to undermine, rather than undergird, the faith of those they teach.

In light of this degeneration of leadership, is it any wonder that moral authority and real relevance frequently are missing as the church confronts the world? Reformation and renewal must begin with those responsible for moral and spiritual leadership.

BLESSED ADVENT

The other main theme of Malachi's prophecy is that of advent. In some liturgical traditions, the advent season encompasses the four Sundays preceding Christmas. During this time, hymns and Scripture readings focus on the first coming of the Saviour, as well as on His return as Judge at the end of time. The wonderful medieval hymn, "O Come, O Come Emmanuel," set to a lovely melody in a minor key, contains references applicable to both advents of the Redeemer.

The Purpose of Advent. Foretold by the prophets and narrated by the evangelists, the birth of Jesus Christ is no pointless prodigy. Malachi unfolds the purpose of the Messiah's advent with striking clarity.

First, he says, the Lord will come to purify His people from the pollution of sin. Only as they are thus refined will they be fit to serve in God's holy presence (Mal. 3:1-4). Second, He will come to punish the disobedient and impenitent for their sins against God and each other. Immorality, idolatry, injustice, and intemperance are not matters of indifference to Him (3:5). The coming Lord also will preserve His people. They shall not be consumed, for He remains forever faithful to His promise of grace (3:6).

The prophet sums up the purpose of the Messiah's advent in terms of both judgment and enlightenment. In other words, He will come to judge the attitudes as well as the actions of all men on that day (4:1); but He also will rise like the heartening sun, warming, illumining, and healing His beloved people (4:2).

The Preparation for Advent. Many people prepare to celebrate the Messiah's coming by decorating their homes and stores with lights and tinsel. Others rehearse in choirs and present special music in praise of the Saviour born at Bethlehem. Yet Malachi also describes how God has prepared for the Messiah's advent (4:3-6). That preparation involves the Law and the Prophets. Malachi specifically refers to the Law of Moses and the mission of Elijah in this instance:

• The moral law given through Moses reveals God's requirements and exposes our failure to meet them to perfection. It condemns us and leads us to Christ as our only hope for pardon and power to obey (Mal. 4:4-5; Gal. 3:22-24).
• The ministry of Elijah also prepares the way for Him who is the Way. In the spirit of Elijah, who denounced idolatry without compromise, John the Baptist will call a wayward generation back to God. In the moral wilderness of this world, he will serve as the herald of the coming Messiah (Mal. 4:4-5; Matt. 11:7-15; Luke 1:16-17).

It is interesting to note that the two men with whom Christ met on the mount of transfiguration were Moses and Elijah. Together, they discussed the central event of the drama of redemption: Jesus' death on the cross. Yet the apostles who were eyewitnesses to that majestic transfiguration focused the eyes of their faith on Jesus alone (Matt. 17:8). Shouldn't our faith be fixed on Him as well?

John Calvin concluded his lectures on the minor prophets with a prayer that we can make our own:

Grant, Almighty God, that as nothing is omitted by Thee to help us onward in the course of our faith, and as our sloth is such that we hardly advance one step though stimulated by Thee—O grant, that we may strive to profit more by the various helps which Thou hast provided for us, so that the Law, the Prophets, the voice of John the Baptist, and especially the doctrine of Thine only-begotten Son, may more fully awaken us, that we may not only hasten to Him, but also proceed constantly in our course, and persevere in it until we shall at length obtain the victory and the crown of our calling, as Thou hast promised an eternal inheritance in heaven to all who faint not but wait for the coming of the Great Redeemer. Amen. (*Commentaries on the Minor Prophets,* Calvin Translation Society, vol. 5, p. 632).

Epilogue

God has spoken through His holy prophets. Their writings, inspired by the Holy Spirit, are now ours to study and believe and obey. As Paul has noted:

> For everything that was written in the past was written to teach us, so that through endurance and the encouragement of the Scripture we might have hope (Rom. 15:4).

Therefore, it is to our benefit to review the major themes of the minor prophets, and to commit ourselves to the truths they reveal and the duties they declare.

Theological reflections are clearly evident in these prophetic writings. We encounter the eternal God, awesome in His majesty. The magnificence of the Lord who created and rules the universe, the eternity and infinity of the One who alone possesses immortality, the grandeur of the Lord God Almighty—this is what we perceive in the prophets. But we also meet the God of the covenant who is faithful to His promises and who pleads for the return of the wayward. The prophets proclaim His loving-kindness no less than His lordship.

Christological passages abound in the minor prophets. They predict the advent of the Messiah who is a tender shepherd, faithful priest, and righteous King. They describe His wisdom, meekness, justice, and benevolence. Their words foretell His base betrayal, cruel suffering, atoning death, and glorious exaltation. These prophets challenge us to welcome Him who came in fulfillment of their prophecies, and who will come again at the end of time to judge the quick and the dead.

Evangelical emphases also are prominent in these books. Though the prophets expose the true nature of sin—whether

137

it be an act or an attitude, directed against God or man—they also invite sinners to repentance. Even their stern words of warning are evidence of the grace of God. Through them, the Lord calls an alienated people home to His welcoming heart of love. If we turn to Him, we will find Him already there. And having found Him, we must make Him known to others, so that the earth may be filled with the knowledge of His glory.

Ethical considerations meet us everywhere in these writings. We are reminded repeatedly about the requirements of a holy God. He summons us to sanctity. Holiness and righteousness are not electives for the elect, but characteristics that must be found in all God's people. Whether in family life or business dealings, we are to prove that our lifestyles are distinctively different from those of persons who do not know the Lord. Can we be indifferent to economic oppression, racial discrimination, political tyranny, and institutionalized crime, and still profess to be followers of Him who hates every crooked way?

Ecclesiastical references are by no means absent from these prophecies. When God's spokesmen reprove Israel's formal ritualism and lack of genuine piety, they are saying something that also is relevant to the church of our day. Whenever idols and ideologies are enshrined in the place that belongs to the Lord alone, or the priests of alien cults are allowed to profane the sanctuary, the sharp sword of the Spirit must cut through this pretended religiosity. The prophets are irrevocably opposed to mere "churchianity."

Of course, the minor prophets do not advocate the idea that the people of God can enjoy a "spiritual" existence in this world without buildings, budgets, plans, programs, committees, and officers. The prophets do not press for the abolition of the temple or synagogue. What they *do* protest is satisfaction with ecclesiastical structures—religious organizations—as a substitute for participation in a spiritual life which is dependent on the Spirit of God and devoted to the Lord of the covenant. This prophetic protest is most necessary in our time. Are we listening?

Eschatological utterances are heard from the lips of these holy men. We listen to warnings of catastrophic judgment on sin and urgent pleas for sinners to return to the pardoning God while there is time. The minor prophets' fiery enthusiasm and impassioned eloquence tell of a kingdom of abundant peace, where righteousness shall flourish and everyone will rest securely. The future is bright with the promises of the sovereign God. But the hope set before us calls for a renewal of holiness in this present hour.

Personal directives come to us from these prophets with precision and power, penetrating the heart and piercing the conscience. They shatter the pride of our egos, disturb the complacency of our spirits, and strip away the pretense behind which we hide. They make us aware of our dismal records and abysmal failure to live up to the light of revelation. They invite us to repentance and encourage our confidence in Him who is everlastingly true to His promises. They challenge us to demonstrate our convictions through a lifestyle that is disciplined by grace and destined for glory.

Who can help us achieve these goals? We have no confidence in our own abilities to cope with the demands of God. Rather, we must confess that our sufficiency is from Him alone. In His Spirit, we have life.

APPENDIX
A CONCISE DICTIONARY
OF THE MINOR PROPHETS

AARON A descendant of Jacob and Levi, the brother of Moses and Miriam. He served as a spokesman for Moses, even as Moses communicated God's will for Israel (Ex. 4:14-16). Aaron also was the first high priest of Israel (Lev. 8:1—9:22). Though he did not always demonstrate a strong character, Aaron *was* a person through whose ministry the Lord led His people during the subsequent experience in the wilderness (Micah 6:4).

ABRAHAM A notable example of unwavering confidence in the utter faithfulness of the covenant God, from whom the Hebrews took their physical descent. Thus, they were referred to by his name (Micah 7:20) as well as those of his son Isaac (Amos 7:16), and grandson Jacob (Micah 4:2; 7:20).

ACZIB A Judean city, southwest of Adullam, also known as Kezib (Gen. 38:5) and Cozeba (1 Chron. 4:22). Mentioned in Micah as living up to its name, which means "deception" (1:14).

ADMAH This city, whose name signifies "red earth," was located near Gomorrah and was destroyed along with it when God sent down fire and brimstone as an act of judgment (Gen. 10:19; 19:24-28; Deut. 29:23; Hosea 11:8).

ADULLAM Located between the Judean hills and the Mediterranean, this ancient city's name means "retreat" or "refuge," as it sheltered David when he was being hunted by Saul (1 Sam. 22:1-2; 2 Sam. 23:13-17; 1 Chron. 11:15-19). Resettled by the exiles who returned from Babylon, Micah associated it with "the glory of Israel" (Neh. 11:30; Micah 1:15).

ADULTERY Sexual infidelity rooted in selfishness, disruptive of the marriage bond; a violation of the seventh commandment, whether by illicit actions or attitudes (Ex. 20:14; Matt. 5:27-30). Adultery is committed spiritually against the Lord when our affections are alienated from Him and directed to rival idols, ideologies, individuals, or institutions (Hosea 1:2).

AHAB Son of Omri and seventh king of Israel (the Northern Kingdom). He reigned during 873-851 B.C. Politically and militarily, he was successful until defeated and killed in a conflict with the Syrian king Ben-hadad. Ahab, together with his wife, Jezebel, supported idolatry and was dramatically confronted by the Prophet Elijah (1 Kings 18). He also was notorious for covetousness as well as apostasy, and came under the severe judgment of God (1 Kings 21:25; 22:34). Those who follow the idolatrous and greedy practices of the house of Ahab will encounter the same ruin (Micah 6:16).

AHAZ Son of Jotham, and king of Judah (735-715 B.C.), he refused to rely on the assurances of God and looked vainly to the Assyrians for security. This dependence on a pagan power furthered apostasy and ensured ruin, despite the warnings of such prophets as Isaiah, Micah, and Hosea (2 Kings 16; 2 Chron. 28:23-27; Isa. 7:1-14; Hosea 1:1; Micah 1:1).

AMARIAH Son of Hezekiah the king, and great-grandfather of Zephaniah the prophet (Zeph. 1:1).

AMAZIAH Not to be confused with the ninth king of Judah—whose story is found mainly in 2 Kings 14 and 2 Chronicles 25—the Amaziah mentioned in Amos (7:10-17) was a priest of Bethel during the reign of Jeroboam II, who resisted the prophet's call to seek sincerity and righteousness in Israel's religious life.

AMITTAI The father of Jonah, fugitive prophet and reluctant missionary (Jonah 1:1).

AMMON Also known as Ben-ammi, this son of Lot is the ancestor from whom the Ammonites descended. They occupied the region east of the Dead Sea, in the land of Gilead, and were noted for their cruelty and idolatry. They refused to help Israel during a crisis, and came under the judgment of God (Gen. 19:38; 1 Kings 11:7; Jer. 41:5-7; Ezek. 25:1-7; Amos 1:13-15).

AMORITE This mountain-dwelling tribe with an ancient history (Gen. 10:16; 14:1), was once a powerful force in Canaan (Num. 21:13, 26-31). The violent Amorites eventually encountered God's vengeance; He brought about their destruction in the course of His providence (Joshua 10:1—11:14; 1 Kings 9:20-21; Amos 2:9).

AMOS With a name signifying "burden-bearer," it was appropriate that this man should be summoned from his work as a herdsman and farmer to deliver a weighty message to the people of Israel during the reign of Uzziah in Judah (779-740 B.C.) and Jeroboam II in the Northern Kingdom (783-743 B.C.). Amos vigorously and courageously protested against religious ritual which was divorced from social righteousness and personal integrity. He sternly warned that impenitence would inevitably lead to the revelation of God's wrath.

ARABAH This term refers to the steppe or desert plain north and south of the Dead Sea. Caravans came through it, and wherever there was water, settlements arose. From its mines, Solomon obtained iron and copper during the time when he ruled over Edom (Josh. 18:18; 2 Sam. 2:29; 4:7; 2 Kings 25:4; Zech. 14:10).

ARAM The northwestern region of Mesopotamia, not to be confused with a district of the hill country related to Gilead (1 Chron. 2:23); sometimes referred to as Syria (Num. 23:7; 2 Sam. 8:5; Hosea 12:12; Amos 1:5). The Arameans, like the Hebrews, were a Semitic people. Their mutual history is marked alternately by cooperation and conflict.

ASHDOD A fortified city of the Philistines, along with Gaza, Ashkelon, Gath, and Ekron (Josh. 13:3) Its religion—marked by the worship of Dagon the fish god—was exposed as false in a memorable confrontation with the ark of the covenant (1 Sam. 5:1-7). Amos predicted the destruction of this pagan power, which came to pass with the invasion of Sargon II of Assyria (Amos 1:8).

ASHKELON This Philistine stronghold was located on the Mediterranean coast approximately twelve miles northeast of Gaza. The prophets denounced it for waging war with the Edomites and the Phoenicians against Israel (Amos 1:6-8; Zech. 9:5). Zephaniah predicted that someday the Jews would occupy the site of Ashkelon (2:4, 7).

ASSYRIA Noted for commercial drive and military might, this expansionist power fought frequently with neighboring countries. Invasion, siege, deportation, and the exaction of tribute were among its tactics. Through the destruction of Sennacherib in 700 B.C., and the fall of Nineveh in 612 B.C., the power of the Assyrians was broken (2 Kings 9—10; 15:29; 16:9; 17:6-41; 18:13—19:37). Many of the minor prophets—as well as Isaiah, Jeremiah, and Ezekiel—refer to Assyria in their writings.

ATTRIBUTES OF GOD The Lord revealed in the minor prophets is the Maker of heaven and earth, who also created a people for His own glory (Hos. 8:14). He rules the world in the course of His providence. In the story of Jonah, for example, He sends a storm, provides a great fish to swallow the fugitive prophet, commands the fish to disgorge him, provides a vine to shelter him, then sends a worm to gnaw at the vine and a blast of heat to chastise His sulking servant (Jonah 1:4, 17; 2:10; 4:6-8). The Lord is holy and righteous in all His ways (Hab. 1:12-13). He exposes sin and executes judgment, like a sudden flash of lightning accompanied by thunder (Hosea 2:10-13; 6:6; 8:14; Joel 2:11). He roars like a lion and devours like a bear (Hosea 11:10; 13:8; 5:13-14). He disciplines disobedience and destroys by the power of His words (Hosea 5:2; 6:5). The Lord is concerned about justice, mercy, and humility (Micah 6:6-8; Amos 5:21-24), and is everlastingly opposed to all oppression (Amos 3:13-15; 5:12-15). This same God is gracious, speaking tenderly, showing compassion, and abounding in love (Hosea 2:14; Joel 2:13; Jonah 4:11). He ransoms from the grave and redeems from death (Hosea 13:14). He pardons sin, heals wounds, revives, restores, and refreshes (Hosea 6:1-3; Joel 2:13, 21-27; Micah 7:18-20). The Lord instructs, strengthens and defends His people, dwelling among them as a glorious presence forever (Joel 3:21; Zech. 2:5, 10).

BAAL The "master" or "lord" acknowledged by certain heathen tribes. Possession and power were ascribed to these baals or baalim. Their fertility cults included idolatrous, barbarous, and immoral rituals (1 Kings 14:23-24; 18:26-28; Jer. 7:9; 19:5; Hosea 2:8, 13). The repudiation of Baal worship was a sign of conversion and a condition of covenant renewal with the living God (Hosea 2:17-18).

BABYLONIANS Also known as the Chaldeans, and dwelling in central Mesopotamia on the river Euphrates, this people was raised up in the providence of God to chastise the faithless Israelites, and then punished by the sovereign Lord for its arrogance (Hab. 1:5-11; 2:4-5).

BALAAM The son of Beor, from the city of Pethor on the river Euphrates. His unusual story as a diviner who tended to sell his skills to the highest bidder is related in Num. 22:2—24:25; 31:8, 16; Deut. 23:4; Neh. 13:2; Micah 6:5; 2 Peter 2:15; Jude 11; and Rev. 2:14. He exemplifies how a talented man may abuse his gifts and lead people away from God into certain ruin.

BALAK King of Moab, enemy of God's covenant people. He hired Balaam the seer to pronounce a curse on the Israelites (Num. 22—24; Micah 6:5; Rev. 2:14). His aim was to divert the Lord's favor from Israel to the Moabites. Frustrated in this endeavor, he then followed Balaam's evil counsel and seduced the Israelites to commit idolatry.

BASHAN A fertile region east of the Sea of Galilee, stretching from Gilead up to Mt. Hermon. Noted for its cattle and sheep, Bashan is mentioned as the pleasant land in which the messianic shepherd will feed His flock (Deut. 32:14; Ps. 22:12; Micah 7:14).

BEERI The father of Hosea the prophet (Hosea 1:1), not to be confused with a Hittite whose daughter Judith was married to Esau (Gen. 26:34).

BEERSHEBA Meaning "the seventh well" or "the well of seven," this was the southernmost town in the kingdom of Judah. The expression "from Dan to Beersheba" thus indicated the sweep of the country from the south of Judah to the northern edge of the nation of Israel (2 Sam. 3:10). Amos reproved Beersheba for receiving, rather than resisting, the contamination of idolatry from Bethel and Dan (Amos 5:5; 8:14).

BEN-HADAD The Syrians believed that their rulers were lineal descendants of the god Hadad and so called them by a name signifying "son of Hadad." This god, who was associated with thunder and storm, also was known as Rimmon (2 Kings 5:18). Amos prophesied that Israel would go into captivity under the people of Ben-Hadad (Amos 1:4).

BENJAMIN The youngest son of Jacob and Rachel, called Benoni ("son of my sorrow") by his mother, and Benjamin ("son of my right hand") by his father (Gen. 35:17). The tribe descended from him occupied a strategic military and commercial position between the lands allocated to Judah and Ephraim (Josh. 18:11-20). Involved in conflict with them according to the prophet's prediction (Hosea 5:8).

BEREKIAH Signifying "Jehovah blesses," several men bore this name in the Old Testament. One of these was the father of the Prophet Zechariah (Zech. 1:1).

BETHEL Though this place name means "house of God," it became a center for the idolatrous worship of golden calves—complete with priests and altars (1 Kings 12:26-30, 32). The prophets denounced such manifestations of apostasy as a source of corruption (Hosea 4:15; 12:4; Amos 3:14; 4:4-6).

BETH AVEN God would have wanted this town to be called Bethel, which means, "the house of God." Instead, it became Beth Aven, "the house of vanity" because it was the center of idol worship. The place and its practices were denounced by the prophets in no uncertain terms (Hosea 4:15; 5:8; 10:5, 8; Amos 4:4; 5:5).

BETH EDEN "The house of Eden" (Amos 1:5), related to the people who were destroyed by the Assyrians (2 Kings 19:12; Isa. 37:12).

BETH EZEL A place in the Philistine plain, associated with Zaanan and Shaphir (Micah 1:11).

BETH OPHRAH This place name literally means "house of dust" (Micah 1:10).

BETHLEHEM EPHRATHAH Distinguished from the town of Bethlehem in Zebulun (Josh. 19:15), this place was known as the city of David (1 Sam. 17:12, 15; Luke 2:4, 11). Here, in the fullness of time, the Messiah was born. Thus, the prophetic promise was fulfilled (Micah 5:2; Matt. 2:3-6). How appropriate, that He who is the Bread of God, the Bread of Heaven, and the Bread of Life, should be born in a town whose name signifies "house of bread." Ephrathah, incidentally, means "fruitful."

BOZRAH Signifying "sheepfold," this Edomite city was once the residence of its kings (Gen. 36:33). But its palaces and prestige were not immune to the revelation of God's justice (Jer. 49:13, 22; Amos 1:12).

BRANCH This is a messianic title, recalling the fact that from the stump of the fallen tree of David's royal house would come a stem or branch. The Branch is destined to flourish with unfading glory (Isa. 11:1-9; Jer. 23:5-6; Zech. 3:8; 6:12).

CALNEH The founding of Calneh, like that of Babel, Erech, and Akkad, is ascribed to Nimrod (Gen. 10:10). This city, in the land of Shinar (southern Mesopotamia), is mentioned in Amos 6:2.

CANAANITE While the descendants of Canaan, a son of Ham, are called Canaanites (Gen. 9—10), the term usually refers to the people who were in the land of Canaan when Joshua led the Israelites in its conquest. The fact that the Canaanites were not completely subdued compromised Israel's military and moral security in subsequent centuries. The prophet's eschatological vision is one in which the Canaanite presence will no longer profane the Lord's house (Zech. 14:21).

CAPHTOR The Mediterranean island of Crete, from which the Philistines probably migrated to west Asia (Jer. 47:4;

Ezek. 25:16; Amos 9:7; Zeph. 2:5;).

CARMEL A beautiful and fruitful area of Palestine, west of the Sea of Galilee and north of the plain of Sharon (Isa. 35:2). The blasting of its pastures and the withering of its freshness illustrate the intensity of divine judgment on sinful nations (Amos 1:2).

COVENANT An agreement, arrangement, alliance, pact or contract initiated by God in His sovereign grace; involves divine promises and confirmation; requires our response of faith and obedience toward the Lord; results in the reality of a relationship in which He is our God and we are His people. The covenant is broken by sin, but restored through Jesus Christ whose atoning sacrifice effected reconciliation. Through faith in Him, we experience peace with God and a new covenantal relationship (Gen. 9:9-17; 15:12-20; 17:1-9; Hosea 2:18; 6:7; 8:1; Mal. 2:4-5, 8, 10, 14; 3:1; Luke 22:20; Heb. 10:15-18; 13:20-21).

CUSH Though Gen. 2:13 implies a west Asian location, other references point to the region of the upper Nile, or southern Egypt, known also as Nubia (Nahum 3:9; Amos 9:7; Zeph. 2:12; 3:10). Not even such a remote land shall be beyond the reach of the arm of God when He moves to judge or save.

CUSHAN Mentioned in Hab. 3:7; may refer to the ancient Midianites, a nomadic people associated with Syria.

DAMASCUS The capital of Syria, and thus representative of a heathen power opposed to Israel and Judah at various times in its long history. Denounced as violent and deserving of destruction by the Lord (Amos 1:3).

DAN The northernmost city of Palestine, where Jeroboam I set up the golden calf for idolatrous worship (1 Kings 12). Threatened with destruction for devotion to false gods (Amos 8:14).

DARIUS King of Persia, whose father conquered the Chaldeans and prepared the way for the Babylonian exiles to return to

Jerusalem and rebuild its walls and temple (Ezra 6:1-15). During his reign, Haggai and Zechariah, prophets of the restoration, exercised their ministry of challenge and encouragement (Hag. 1:1-10; Zech. 1:1).

DAVID The shepherd-king of Israel, upon whose house God promised to pour out the Spirit of grace and supplication, so that people would look on Him whom they pierced, and mourn for Him (Zech. 12:12; John 19:31-37).

DAY OF THE LORD As described in passages such as Amos 8:9-10 and Zeph. 1:14-18, this dreadful day signals the advent of the Lord to final judgment. All previous manifestations of His displeasure against unrighteousness and ungodliness are a prelude to that climactic revelation of His wrath.

DIBLAIM The mother of Gomer, who married Hosea the prophet (Hosea 1:3).

DIVINATION Diviners who try to gain secret knowledge through trances or the interpretation of omens, rather than relying on revelation from God, are subject to His displeasure and condemnation (Hosea 4:12; Micah 3:5-7). We must listen for guidance to what the Spirit says in the Scriptures, rather than depend on subjective feelings, horoscopes, or astrology.

EDOM The land of Esau and his descendants, the Edomites (Gen. 25:30; 36:1, 8). By the thirteenth century B.C., Edom had kings (Gen. 36:31-39). For opposing and harassing the covenant people, the Edomites were threatened with irrevocable doom (Joel 3:19; Amos 1:11; Obad. 10-14).

EGYPT The land of the pharaohs played an important part in biblical history and is not altogether excluded from scriptural prophecy. In the minor prophets, Egypt is mentioned as an untrustworthy ally and a cruel adversary marked for desolation (Hosea 7:11; Joel 3:19).

EKRON The most northern of the Philistine Pentapolis, situated on the border between Dan and Judah, it followed the cult of Baal-zebub (2 Kings 1:3) and was denounced by the prophets of God (Amos 1:8; Zeph. 2:4; Zech. 9:5, 7).

EPHAH In the system of weights and measures used during Old Testament times, the *ephah* was a container large enough to hold a person (Zech. 5:6-10). It was employed to measure out cereals with exactness (Amos 8:5; Micah 6:10) as a matter of economic justice.

EPHOD A "covering" or "outer garment," the shoulder vestment worn by Hebrew priests. On the pectoral or breastplate, there were twelve precious stones, each inscribed with the name of one of the tribes of Israel (Ex. 25:7; 28:4, 12, 16; Hosea 3:4).

EPHRAIM A son of Joseph (Gen. 41:50-52), ho became the ancestor of two tribes: Ephraim and Manasseh, which feuded fiercely among themselves (Isa. 9:20-21). Eventually, Ephraim took a leading role in the rebellion that led to the formation of the Northern Kingdom. That kingdom, usually called Israel, also was known as Ephraim because of the prominence of that tribe in its affairs (Hosea 5:3; 9:3-16).

ESAU Born to Isaac and Rebecca, and the older twin of Jacob (Gen. 25:24-25), he showed a foolish scale of values in trading away his birthright for a bowl of stew. The name Esau also indicated the land of Edom, where his descendants dwelt. At least one prophet predicted the doom of Edom in retribution for its sins (Obad. 6, 8-9).

EUPHRATES Often referred to in Scripture as "the river" or "the great river," it flowed from the mountains of Armenia for hundreds of miles to the Persian Gulf. It served as the border between the Assyrians and the Hittites after the Solomonic era. Micah refers to this river in a prophecy about the expanding kingdom of God (Micah 7:12).

GATH Part of the Philistine Pentapolis, inhabited by giants like Goliath (Josh. 13:3; 1 Sam. 17:4; 2 Sam. 21:19-22). The prophet used the fall of this walled city to warn those at ease in Zion that their complacency would be shattered by defeat and deportation (Amos 6:1-2).

GAZA An important Philistine trading center on the edge of a desert region, threatened with fiery destruction for its many transgressions (Amos 1:6-7). The site would be left desolate (Zeph. 2:4), and the king of Gaza slain (Zech. 9:5). These prophecies were fulfilled, first through an Egyptian Pharaoh (Jer. 47:1), and then by the invasion of Alexander the Great in 332 B.C.

GEBA A town associated with the military exploits of Jonathan (1 Sam. 13:3; 14:5). Later the northernmost stronghold of the kingdom of Judah (2 Kings 23:8; 2 Chron. 16:6). Mentioned in the prophecy of Zechariah concerning the region from Geba to Rimmon (Zech. 14:10).

GEDALIAH The grandfather of Zephaniah the prophet (Zeph. 1:1).

GIBEAH Since the term means "mountain" or "hill," it is understandable that several Palestinian towns were called by this name. One of these was in the territory of Benjamin (1 Sam. 13:2), where a sanctuary was maintained. King Saul was a native of Gibeah (1 Sam. 11:4). Mentioned in a prediction of conflict and desolation by Hosea (Hosea 5:8; 9:9; 10:9).

GILEAD The region south of the Sea of Galilee and north of the Dead Sea, noted for its rugged hills, fertile fields, and dense forests. The balm of Gilead was known for its curative powers (Gen. 37:25; Jer. 8:22; 46:11, 51:8; Ezek. 27:17). The people of Gilead are accused of shameful crimes and denounced as wicked and worthless (Hosea 6:8; 12:11). Yet the Lord also takes vengeance on Ammon for ripping open the pregnant women of Gilead, and on Damascus for its cruel treatment of the inhabitants there (Amos 1:3, 13). The messianic shepherd will lead His flock to the green meadows of Gilead in the time of restoration (Micah 7:14; Zech. 10:10).

GILGAL A "circle." Cities surrounded with a circle or wall of stones were sometimes called Gilgal. One of these was near Bethel; it enshrined an altar/memorial for the observance of heathen rituals revolting to the Lord (Hosea 4:15, 12:11; Amos 4:4).

GOMER The daughter of Diblaim; wife of Hosea and mother

of his three children; faithless to her husband. Her forgiveness by the prophet is illustrative of God's pardoning grace to His wayward people (Hosea 3:1).

GOMORRAH One of the five "cities of the plain," at the southern end of the Dead Sea, notorious for its godlessness and immorality, and destroyed by fire and brimstone from the skies (Gen. 19:1-29). The same destiny of doom awaits all those who partake of Gomorrah's sins, even though they may possess the heritage of the Law and the Prophets (Amos 4:11).

GREEKS The Lord rebuked Tyre and Sidon for plundering Jerusalem's templo and selling Judah's inhabitants to the Greeks. The Lord promised to deliver His people from that oorvitude in exile (Joel 3:6; Zech. 9:13).

HABAKKUK Did he prophesy during the reign of Manasseh, or that of Jehoram? Does his name mean "embrace" or is it related to the Akkadian term for a trailing plant? Of this we can be certain: Habakkuk's prophecy, cast in the form of a dialogue between the Lord and the prophet, deals with a philosophy of history. While the Lord may allow the ungodly to chastise His people, He will also preserve those whose faith remains in Him.

HADAD RIMMON A place in the valley of Megiddo named for two Syrian divinities. Here the godly young King Josiah was mortally wounded and great lamentations were made over his death (2 Kings 23:29-30; Zech. 12:11).

HADRACH A land mentioned along with Damascus and Hamath, against whom the severity of the Lord's word is directed by the prophet (Zech. 9:1).

HAGGAI In partnership with Zechariah, he encouraged the Jewish governor, Zerubbabel, and the high priest, Joshua, in the work of restoring the temple after the return from Babylon. His ministry, begun in 520 B.C., was necessary because the initial enthusiasm of the returned exiles to rebuild the temple had waned and their attention was diverted to concerns of lesser value.

HAMATH A land bordering on Hadrach and Damascus; threatened by the Lord with the irrevocable loss of its power and possessions on account of its transgressions (Zech. 9:2). The destruction of "great Hamath" was to serve as a warning to the complacent in Zion who enjoyed a false sense of security (Amos 6:2).

HAZAEL An official of Ben-hadad, king of Syria, who discussed the illness and possible recovery of that monarch with Elisha. Hazael eventually murdered Ben-hadad and usurped the throne (2 Kings 8:7-15). The dates of his reign are estimated as 841-798 B.C., and those years were marked by many raids against Israel (2 Kings 13:22). For all this, destruction would come to him and Syria in the providence of God (Amos 1:4).

HELDAI Returning from the exile in Babylon with his friends, he brought silver and gold to Jerusalem for the fashioning of a crown and the restoration of the temple (Zech. 6:9).

HEN This name, meaning "the gracious one," recalls a person associated with Heldai, Tobijah, and Jedaiah as a custodian of the crown to be kept in the temple of the Lord (Zech. 6:9-14).

HEZEKIAH "The Lord has strengthened." This king reigned in Judah (724-695 B.C.), and the details of his rule are recorded in 2 Kings 18—20, 2 Chron. 29—32, and Isa. 36—39. After allowing the people to follow idolatrous rituals, he restored the temple and reinstituted the Passover. As part of his reforming work, heathen altars were destroyed (2 Chron. 30). One of the prophets who spoke for God and encouraged reform during Hezekiah's reign was Hosea (1:1).

HOSEA His name means "Jehovah saves." He was the son of Beeri and served as a spokesman for God in a time of confusion and corruption. Through a domestic tragedy involving a faithless wife, the birth of three children, and tenderness open to restoration, Hosea came to identify with the pain and redemptive purpose of God, as they related to the waywardness of Israel.

IDDO The father of Berekiah and grandfather of Zechariah the prophet (Zech. 1:1, 7).

IDOL Anything or anyone allowed to usurp the place of priority that belongs to God alone. Grotesque images—such as individuals, institutions, and ideologies that deprive Him of preeminence as the decisive factor in shaping attitudes and directing our actions—are to be recognized and repudiated as idols. Failure to do so results inevitably in disordered priorities and destruction (Ex. 20:1-6; Hosea 8:1-6; 9:10; 11:2).

ISAAC The son of Abraham and father of Jacob, indispensable to the continuity and increase of the Hebrew people. The "house of Isaac," or his descendants, are not exempt from the prophetic warning occasioned by disobedience to the will of the Lord (Amos 7:16).

ISRAEL While referring to Jacob, the son of Isaac in the individual sense (Gen. 35:10), it also denotes the *people* of Israel descended from him, as well as the Northern Kingdom of the ten tribes that broke with the Southern Kingdom of Judah. Hosea was one of the prophets who delivered God's message to Israel (Hosea 1:1).

JEBUSITES Inhabitants of Jebus, which later became Jerusalem. Captured by David, it was made the capital of the nation of Israel (Josh. 15:63; 2 Sam. 5:1-9). Zechariah foretold how Ekron, like the Jebusites, would be conquered by divine intervention so as to end the oppression of His people (Zech. 9:7-8).

JEDAIAH Associated with Heldai and Tobijah in bringing silver and gold from Babylon for the rebuilding of the temple during the days of Zerubbabel. He also participated in the coronation of the high priest Joshua (Zech. 6:9-15).

JEHOASH Also known as Joash. Several men in the Old Testament bore this name. One was a godly king in Judah (884-848 B.C.), another ruled in Israel and was a worshiper of idols. During the reign of the latter's son, Jeroboam, in the Northern Kingdom, Amos declared the word of the Lord (Amos 1:1).

JEHOZADAK The father of Joshua, who served as high priest in Jerusalem when Haggai and Zechariah gave fresh impetus to the rebuilding of the temple (Hag. 1:1). Bearing a name whose meaning is "Jehovah is righteous," Jehozadak had been Israel's high priest during much of the Babylonian Captivity (1 Chron. 6:14-15).

JEHU Son of Jehoshaphat, and tenth king of Israel. Hosea prophesied during his reign (842-814 B.C.).

JEROBOAM Hosea, Amos, Joel, and Jonah all prophesied during the reign of Jeroboam II, whose forty-one-year rule began about 785 B.C. It was an era marked by outward prosperity in the Northern Kingdom of Israel/Samaria, but plagued with internal corruption (2 Kings 14:23-24).

JEZREEL The first son born to Hosea and his wife Gomer. His name recalls the massacre committed by the house of Jehu in the Valley of Jezreel and forecasts the judgment of God on the kingdom of Israel because of it (Hosea 1:4-5).

JOASH Also known as Jehoash, he ruled in Israel for about sixteen years, and was succeeded by his son Jeroboam II—in whose time Hosea prophesied (Hosea 1:1).

JOEL The son of Pethuel, whose name means "Jehovah is God," was a senior contemporary of Amos and Hosea during the reign of Jehoash in the ninth century B.C. He prophesied the advent of judgment in apocalyptic terms and announced the descent of the Spirit. This promise was fulfilled at Pentecost (Acts 2:14-21).

JONAH The son of Amittai, sent to warn Nineveh of impending judgment on account of its notorious wickedness. Disobedient and disciplined, he eventually delivered the Lord's message and sulked when the Ninevites repented and were spared by the God of compassion. His book not only is a protest against narrow nationalism, but foretells the death and resurrection of Jesus Christ (Matt. 12:38-42).

JOSHUA Not to be confused with the successor to Moses who led the people of Israel in the conquest of Canaan, this Joshua was the son of Jehozadak and served as high priest during the rebuilding of the temple (Hag. 1:1; 2:1-5).

JOSIAH King of Judah (639-609 B.C.), this son of Amon and grandson of Manasseh repudiated the polytheism of his predecessors and led a movement of reform in his realm. This religious revival was sparked by the rediscovery of the book of the Law of God in the rubble of the temple (2 Kings 22—23; 2 Chron. 34—35). Zephaniah was one who prophesied in the days of this young and godly king (Zeph. 1:1).

JOTHAM Son of King Uzziah, Jotham reigned in Judah during the prophetic ministry of Isaiah, Hosea, and Micah (Hosea 1:1; Micah 1:1).

JUDAH When the United Kingdom ruled by David and Solomon was split in the tumultuous times of Rehoboam, the northern tribes became the kingdom of Israel while the two southern tribes comprised the kingdom of Judah. It was to Judah that Amos, Hosea, and Micah—like Isaiah—primarily proclaimed their prophetic messages.

KERIOTH Distinguished from another Kerioth also known as Hazor and located in southern Judah (Josh. 15:25), the one mentioned in Amos (2:1-3) is a leading city of Moab and a target for the flaming arrows of divine judgment.

KIR A walled town in which captives were kept (Amos 1:5).

KISLEV The ninth month of the Jewish year, corresponding to December. It marked the time when Zechariah received the word of the Lord during the fourth year of the reign of Darius (Zech. 7:1).

LACHISH A fortified Canaanite city thirty-one miles southwest of Jerusalem, it once served as the headquarters of Sennacherib (702 B.C.). From its excavated ruins come "the Lachish letters," which are the oldest known Hebrew inscriptions. Micah denounced the inhabitants of Lachish for their corrupting influence on the people of Israel (Micah 1:13).

LAST DAYS This expression refers to the era of messianic blessing, inaugurated with the Incarnation, and destined to conclude when Christ returns in power and glory at the last day (Joel 2:28-32; Micah 4:1-5; Heb. 1:1-2; 2 Peter 3:1-14).

LAW OF THE LORD Divine revelation designed to give us an authoritative standard for conduct, governing our relationships to God and one another (Ex. 20:1-17; Matt. 22:34-40). Disobedience to His revealed will, whether by action or attitude, betrays corruption and calls down condemnation (Amos 2:4-5).

LEBANON A Hebrew word meaning "white," applied to the snow-capped mountain range and its adjacent region north of Galilee. Renowned for its forests of cypress and cedar (Hosea 14:5-6).

LEVI The house of Levi, descended from Jacob's third son by Leah (Gen. 29:34; 35:22-26), a tribe appointed to priestly service (Ex. 2:1-10; 6:14-27; Num. 26:59), sharing with the rest of God's people in sorrow for the pierced Messiah (Zech. 12:10-14).

LIBYA The land of the Lubim, descendants of Ham (Gen. 10:13); west of Egypt, on Africa's northern coast; mentioned as an ally of an impressive kingdom, it still was not immune to judgment (Nahum 3:9).

LO-AMMI The third child born to Hosea and Gomer, whose name means "not my people" and points to the fact that the Lord disowns those who refuse to acknowledge Him as their God (Hosea 1:8-9). The grand reversal of grace is experienced when those who are not worthy to be His people, are embraced by His love and they confess Him as their God (Hosea 2:23; 1 Peter 2:9-10).

LO DEBAR An obscure town in Gilead east of the Jordan, related to the story of David and Mephibosheth (2 Sam. 9:1-13). Mentioned in Amos 6:13.

LO-RUHAMAH The second child born to Hosea and Gomer. Her name means "not loved" or "not pitied," symbolic of the fact that Israel will be shown the severity, rather than the goodness, of God on account of its sins (Hosea 1:6-7).

MALACHI Protesting against mixed marriages, devastating divorces, irreverent priests, blemished sacrifices, and persistent idolatry, Malachi was a living exposition of his name ("My messenger"). This spokesman for God also communicated a message both evangelical and eschatological. The Lord would not forget those who revere Him, and the rising of the Sun of Righteousness was sure to dispel the darkness of ignorance, sin, and death.

MARESHAH A strategic Judean city fortified by Rehoboam (2 Chron. 11:5-12); God would execute His justice against it (Micah 1:15).

MAROTH A place whose inhabitants are pictured as writhing in pain as they suffer the discipline of disaster from the hand of the Lord (Micah 1:12).

MEGIDDO Located in a mountainous region, scene of several tragic events. Ahaziah of Judah died here after being wounded in a struggle with Jehu (2 Kings 9:27). At Megiddo, godly King Josiah also perished after intervening in a conflict between the Egyptians and Assyrians (2 Kings 23:29-30). The mourning over Josiah's death provides the background for the prophecy about people mourning for the pierced Messiah (Zech. 12:10-14). The name "Megiddo" has been incorporated into *har-megiddon*, hill of Megiddo, rendered as Armageddon in the New Testament (Rev. 16:16).

MICAH His name asked the question, "Who is like Jehovah?" and his prophecy provided an answer to it. Micah reveals a God whose holiness and righteousness react to sin at every level of society. He also points to the coming of Christ, the shepherd-king, and makes known the pardoning grace of the incomparable God.

MIDIANITES Desert dwellers and camel riders who conspired with the Moabites to have Balaam curse Israel and lead the Israelites into idolatry and immorality (Num. 22; 25). They also combined with the Amorites on one occasion and the Amalekites on another, to oppose Israel. The prophet predicts their anguish at the approach of the Holy One (Hab. 3:7).

MIZPAH Several localities shared this name in the Old Testament. One of these was fortified by Asa of Judah against Baasha of Israel in a conflict involving Syria (1 Kings 15:22; 2 Chron. 16:6). Hosea refers to Mizpah in a warning to the priests, princes, and people of Israel (Hosea 5:1).

MOAB A fertile plain east of the Dead Sea, inhabited by a people related to Israel, yet hostile to the Israelites. The Moabites were defeated by Ehud (Jud. 3:12) and David (2 Sam. 8:2). They eventually were subjugated by the Assyrians. Amos prophesied concerning Moab and its impending doom (Amos 2:1).

MORESHETH The hometown of the Prophet Micah, located about twenty miles southwest of Jerusalem (Micah 1:1, 14).

MOUNT PARAN In the wilderness region of Sinai (Deut. 33:2). The magnificent theophany recorded by Habakkuk portrays God as coming from Teman and descending from Mount Paran with a glory that fills the heavens and a splendor like the sunrise (Hab. 3:3).

NAHUM From the town of Elkosh, Nahum prophesied during the years between the Assyrian capture of Thebes (664-663 B.C.) and the destruction of Nineveh (612 B.C.). The meaning of his name ("Jehovah comforts") also describes the contents of his prophecy: The Lord comforts His people by punishing their oppressors with irrevocable loss.

NAMES OF GOD In the minor prophets, God is called "the Lord" (Hosea 1:1); "the Most High" (Hosea 11:7); "the Holy One" (Hosea 11:9); "the Lord your God" (Hosea 12:9); "your helper" (Hosea 13:9); "the Almighty" (Joel 1:15); "the sovereign Lord" (Amos 1:8); "my holy One" (Hab. 1:12); "rock" (Hab. 1:12); "God my Saviour" (Hab. 3:18); "my strength" (Hab. 3:18). There also are references to "the Spirit of the Lord" (Micah 3:8); "the desired of all nations" (Hag. 2:7); "the branch" (Zech. 3:8); and the "sun of righteousness" (Mal. 4:2). We should remember that these names are more than identifying labels or formal titles. They actually describe the character of God and His relationship to us. They are, therefore, revelatory of His nature and purpose. Each should be considered a gem to be treasured.

NATHAN This prophet once courageously confronted David with his notorious moral failure. But by Zechariah's time, both the descendants of David and the house of Nathan are described as contemplating the One whom they have pierced and mourning for Him bitterly (Zech. 12:12).

NAZIRITES Not to be confused with the Nazarenes, inhabitants of Nazareth (Acts 2:22) or followers of Jesus the Nazarene (Acts 24:5), the Nazirites were people consecrated to God by a vow of separation and voluntary abstinence for a religious purpose (Num. 6:1-23). This vow could last from thirty days to a lifetime. It involved abstaining from wine (and even grapes), foregoing the use of a razor, and avoiding contact with corpses. Amos protests against the Israelites for having disregarded the spiritual teaching and personal example of the Nazirites (Amos 2:11-12).

NEGEV This transliterated Hebrew word meaning "dry" also is the name of the desert region south of Judea. Here Hagar encountered God's messenger (Gen. 16:7, 14). Isaac and Jacob dwelt in the Negev for a time (Gen. 24:62; 37:1). This was the setting for some of David's heroic deeds (1 Sam. 27:5-6). Obadiah refers to it in his vision of the future (Obad. 19-20).

NEW MOONS The terms "month" and "moon" were used synonymously in the times of Moses (Ex. 19:1). The appearance of the new moon not only served as a measurement of time, but also as an occasion of worship. After the exile, for instance, on the first day of the seventh month (Tishri: October), the start of a new year was marked by the blowing of trumpets, the public reading of God's Law, and widespread rejoicing. When this observance became a mere formality, the Lord rejected it as strongly as He condemned the idolatrous practice of worshiping the moon itself (2 Kings 23:5; Jer. 8:2; Hosea 1:11).

NILE The prophet uses Egypt's great river to describe God's dealings with a sinful people. As the river rises in flood and then its waters recede, so shall it be with the land destined for divine judgment. The destruction of a swelling tide shall be followed by desolation as the waters ebb (Amos 8:8).

NIMROD Mentioned in Gen. 10:8-12 as a mighty hunter, regarded as the founder of the Babylonian and Assyrian empires, the land of Nimrod, declared the prophet, might invade the borders of Jacob. But the victory would go to the divinely provided leader and shepherd who saves His people (Micah 5:1-6).

NINEVEH The great city of ancient Assyria, renowned for its military conquests, ingenuity, aggressiveness, and arrogance. Warned of impending destruction through the preaching of Jonah, it repented and received a suspended sentence. Eventually, Nineveh was punished for its resumed transgressions (Jonah 1:1-2; 3:1-10; Nahum 1:1; 3:19).

OBADIAH At least a dozen men in the Old Testament were named Obadiah ("servant of Jehovah"). The most familiar of these was a prophet whose exact date is uncertain. It is unclear whether he prophesied during the reign of Ahab, Jehoram, Ahaz, or even after the capture of Jerusalem by the Chaldeans in 587 B.C. There is no doubt, however, concerning the message conveyed by his vigorous poetry: The certainty of divine judgment and the inevitability of God's ultimate triumph.

OMRI His brief but notorious reign (886-874 B.C.?) is chronicled in 1 Kings 16:15-28. His story is one of wars, murders, revolutions, sieges, and suicides. Omri's son, Ahab, married Jezebel, princess of Tyre, with ruinous results for the religious life of Israel. The prophet denounced those who "observed the statutes of Omri" and engaged in practices abhorrent to the Almighty (Micah 6:16).

ORION References to astronomy are not lacking in the Scriptures. The Lord asked Job if he could bind the chains of the Pleiades or loose the cords of Orion, and Amos refers to these constellations as well (Amos 5:8).

PHILISTIA The plain of Palestine inhabited by the Philistines, who probably migrated there eastward across the Mediterranean from the island of Caphtor or Crete during the thirteenth century B.C. The Philistine Pentapolis comprised Ashdod, Gaza, Ashkelon, Ekron, and Gath (Josh. 13:3; 1 Sam.

6:17), ruled by five "Lords of the Philistines." They prospered because of their knowledge of metal working, and worshiped idols such as Dagon, Astarte, and Baalzebub (1 Sam. 31:10; 2 Kings 1:2,6, 16). These cities struggled constantly with the people of Israel. For acts of oppression and sacrilege, Philistia was condemned by the Lord (Joel 3:4-7).

PLEIADES The star cluster of the Pleiades, mentioned along with Orion in Job (38:31), also is referred to in Amos (5:8) as the prophet proclaims the greatness of the Lord.

PRIEST As the prophet represented God to people and brought them His truth, so the priest represented sinners before the Lord and offered sacrifice and prayers of intercession on their behalf. Corrupt priests misled the people from the path of devotion, and brought upon themselves divine retribution (Hosea 4:9; Micah 3:11-12).

PUT A nation identified with Libya, renowned for its adept use of the shield in battle (Nahum 3:9; Jer. 46:9). But as the allies of Put had no sure defense against attack, so Nineveh would have no secure refuge in the day of the revelation of God's justice.

RABBAH A city of the Ammonites, besieged by David and captured when Joab gained access to its water supply. The prophets denounced the idolatry of Rabbah and prophesied its fiery destruction ((Jer. 49:2-6; Ezek. 21:20; Amos 1:14).

REDEMPTION The release of a captive by the payment of a ransom. The Lord wants to liberate His people from servitude (Hosea 7:13). As He set Israel free from the bondage of Egypt through the Exodus, so He delivers His elect from the penalty and power of sin through the Redeemer (Mark 10:45; Gal. 1:4; 3:13).

REGEM-MELECH He accompanied Sharezer on his journey from Bethel to Jerusalem to ask the priests and prophets about the value of fasting (Zech. 7:1-3).

REMNANT Among the people of God descended from Abraham, and externally marked by circumcision or attendance at temple and synagogue, a remnant exists that has a spiritual relationship with the Lord and survives the winnowing of chastisement. God has mercy on the remnant of Jacob, and He deals mercifully with the remnant of Joseph. He continues the godly line even when the majority seems apostate because He is faithful to His covenant promises (Amos 5:15; Micah 5:7-8; Mal. 3:6).

RETURN A key term in the biblical understanding of the human condition and the essence of conversion. By nature, we are egocentric rather than God-centered. Willfully, foolishly, fatally we pursue our own way. Our only hope is to return to the Lord and seek His pardoning grace (Hosea 6:1).

REVIVAL Spiritual recovery is not the result of human resolve; rather, it is a blessing of God's sovereign grace. He alone is the Lord and Giver of life who revives and restores (Hosea 6:2; Hab. 3:1-2). Real revival usually is related to the rediscovery of God's authoritative Word, repentance and confession of sin, fervent prayer, and willing obedience to the living Lord.

RIMMON Zechariah predicted that the whole land, from Geba to Rimmon south of Jerusalem, would someday become like the Arabah (Zech. 14:10). It would be turned into a steppe or desert plain.

SABBATH The weekly day of rest and worship (Ex. 20:8-11), commemorating God's contemplative rest from His creative labors (Gen. 1:1—2:3) and celebrating Israel's divine deliverance from bondage through the Exodus (Deut. 5:15). Amos remarked that some people were impatient for the Sabbath observance to end, so that they could resume their profiteering, exploitation, and fraudulent dealings (Amos 8:4-6).

SABEANS The people of Saba, a land related to the Nile, Upper Egypt, and Ethiopia. Tyre and Sidon were warned that their sons and daughters would be sold into slavery and dwell as exiles in the distant country of the Sabeans (Joel 3:8).

SACRIFICE In the prophetic writings, a vigorous emphasis is placed on righteousness and mercy, rather than on the precise and punctual performance of religious rituals. This emphasis does not repudiate the sacrificial system instituted of God in the Mosaic era, but indicts all who are satisfied with outward ceremonies while neglecting sincerity and integrity in life's relationships (Hosea 6:6; Amos 5:21-24; Micah 6:6-8).

SAMARIA The ten tribes led by Jeroboam in secession from the kingdom over which David and Solomon had once reigned, formed a kingdom in the north known as Israel or Samaria. This was the region in which Ahab and Jezebel encouraged a corrupting combination of luxury, vice, violence, and idolatry. Amos, Hosea, and Micah were among the prophets who protested such trends and predicted ruin.

SHAPHIR Also known as Saphir, which signifies "glittering"; a town mentioned in Micah 1:11, and likely located in southwestern Palestine.

SHAREZER Emissary from Bethel, along with Regem-Melech, who questioned the priests and prophets regarding the need to continue formal fasting (Zech. 7:1-3).

SHEALTIEL The father of Zerubbabel, who was governor of Judah during the reconstruction of the temple at Jerusalem (Hag. 1:1; 2:23).

SHEPHERD Like Isaiah and Ezekiel, the minor prophets portrayed the Lord as a shepherd. In contrast to false shepherds who fleece and ravage the flock, God exercises a tender and protective pastoral care for His people. This divine Shepherd is cheaply valued, betrayed, and smitten (Micah 5:1-4; Zech. 11:4-16; 13:7).

SHIMEI At least nineteen men were called by this name in the Old Testament. One, who was a relative of Saul, cursed David as a man of violence (2 Sam. 16:5). It also was the clan name of those who took care of the tabernacle (Num. 3:21). The house of Shimei is mentioned by the prophet as mourning over the contemplation of the pierced Lord (Zech. 12:13).

SIDON A city—as well as a region—of Phoenicia. Famed for artisic metal work, glass blowing, and crimson dye, but infamous for its pagan idolatry and materialism (Isa. 23; Ezek. 28). Threatened with ruin by the Prophet Joel (Joel 3:4).

SODOM Notorious for its violence and immorality, this city was destroyed by divine retribution (Gen. 18:6—19:29). Homosexual acts still are described as "sodomy." Though such practices may be increasingly condoned by secular society and commended by "gay churches," they are unequivocally condemned as sin by Holy Scripture. Like heterosexual deviations from God's moral standard, they deserve His wrath and require the grace of His Gospel (Rom. 1:16-32).

SPIRIT OF THE LORD In contrast to false prophets who were misled by their subjectivity and speculation, God's true messengers are led by the Spirit who fills them with power and justice (Micah 3:8—4:5).

SUN OF RIGHTEOUSNESS As darkness symbolizes spiritual ignorance, sinfulness, and mortality, so the rising of the Sun of Righteousness signals the dawning of a new day. The Messiah's advent brings a clear knowledge of the true God, sure healing for the moral evil that deforms and debilitates personality, and eternal life to those who languish in the land of the shadow of death (Isa. 9:2; Mal. 4:12; John 8:12; Rev. 22:1-5).

TARSHISH When God called Jonah to go eastward to Nineveh, he deliberately headed westward to Tarshish (Jonah 1:3). The runaway prophet soon learned that he could not escape the omnipresent and omnipotent God. Everyone who fails to fulfill a God-appointed task takes a ticket, in effect, to Tarshish.

TEKOA A city of Judah, about twelve miles south of Jerusalem, where Amos was a herdsman until the Lord summoned him to prophesy as His spokesman (Amos 1:1).

TEMAN An Edomite city which is mentioned by Amos as a target of God's fierce and fiery fury (Amos 1:11-12); also referred to by Habakkuk in connection with the majestic manifestation of the glorious Lord (Hab. 3:3).

THEBES Formerly the capital of Egypt. Located on the Nile, famed for the ruins of Karnak and Luxor. As a cult center for the worship of Amon, it was threatened with judgment by Jeremiah (Jer. 46:25) and Ezekiel (Ezek. 30:14-16). The devastation of Thebes is mentioned by Nahum as a warning to Nineveh (Nahum 3:8-10).

TITHES Abraham gave tithes to Melchizedek, the priest of the Most High (Gen. 14:17-20; Heb. 7:4), and Jacob promised to devote a tenth of his possessions to the God who met him at Bethel (Gen. 28:16-22). Payment of a tithe in recognition of His lordship and our stewardship, as well as to express gratitude for the benefits of redemption, is acceptable in God's sight and brings spiritual enrichment. The withholding of such gifts is condemned as a violation of the eighth commandment (Mal. 3:8-12).

TOBIJAH An exile who returned from Babylon with Heldai and Jedaiah with offerings of silver and gold for the reconstruction of the temple in Jerusalem (Zech. 6:9).

TYRE A Phoenician seaport, associated with Sidon. Renowned as a commercial center and maritime power, it accumulated considerable wealth before coming under the domination of Egypt, Babylon, Persia, and Greece in subsequent centuries. Mentioned by Joel (3:4), and Amos (1:9-10).

UZZIAH A king of Judah (769-738 B.C.), also known as Azariah, whose reign was marked by military success and financial prosperity. He captured and fortified the seaport of Elath (2 Kings 14:22) and restored the walls of Jerusalem (2 Chron. 26). Uzziah was stricken with leprosy as a punishment for usurping priestly prerogatives (2 Chron. 26:16). Hosea and Amos were two of the prophets who exercised their ministry in his era.

VALLEY OF AVEN Since the word "aven" signifies vanity, emptiness, idol, or wickedness, the Valley of Aven would be a location detested by the one true and living God. Amos declared that its king faced certain destruction (Amos 1:5).

VALLEY OF JEHOSHAPHAT Since Jehoshaphat means "Jehovah judges," this is the valley in which the nations shall be gathered by the Lord for the revelation of His justice (Joel 3:2, 12). The phrase thus is symbolic of the awesome reality of God's final and universal judgment.

VALLEY OF THE ARABAH The Lord God Almighty declared that He would stir up a nation against the house of Israel. Its oppression would extend from the entrance to Hamath to the valley of the Arabah, as a manifestation of God's displeasure with the sins of His people (Amos 6:14).

WORD OF THE LORD The message that came to the prophets as a revelation from God, communicated faithfully and courageously by His authentic spokesmen (Hosea 1:1; 2 Peter 1:21). This word calls for a response of repentance, faith, and obedience since we are addressed not merely by a human messenger, but by the living God.

ZAANAN A place mentioned by Micah (1:11) in the Shephelah or lowland of Judah.

ZAREPHATH Elijah once lived here during days of drought and famine (1 Kings 17:9). Located north of Palestine, near Tyre and Sidon, it was mentioned in Obadiah 20 to indicate the expansion of the Lord's kingdom.

ZEBOIIM One of the cities in the vale of Siddim destroyed by an act of divine judgment, along with Sodom and Gomorrah (Gen. 14:2, 8; Hosea 11:8); a warning to others who persist in disregarding and defying the revealed will of God.

ZECHARIAH A son of Berekiah, with a name that means "God remembers," this contemporary of Haggai encouraged the returned exiles from Babylon to follow the lead of Zerubbabel and Joshua in the work of rebuilding the temple.

ZEPHANIAH The son of Cushi, and a descendant of Hezekiah the king. He exercised a prophetic ministry during the reign of godly Josiah, king of Judah, and encouraged that youthful monarch in his reforming labors. The prophecy that bears his name predicts the dawning of the dreadful Day of the Lord and concludes on a note of restoration by grace.

ZERUBBABEL The governor of Judah during the reign of
Darius in Persia; son of Shealtiel; associated with Haggai and
Zechariah in the work of rebuilding the temple at Jerusalem
after the return from the Babylonian Exile (Hag. 1:1; 2:23;
Zech. 4:1-14). A dedicated leader who needed encourage-
ment for the fulfillment of the work God gave him to do.

ZION Its original meaning may have been "citadel," but it came
to indicate one of the hills on which an ancient Jebusite
fortress was erected and the city of Jerusalem established.
The name also is used figuratively for the people of God (Joel
2:1, 15; 3:16-17, 21; Pss. 126:1; 129:5; Heb. 12:22; Rev. 14:1).